Get Your Ideas Approved

How to get your boss to approve everything you want to do.

Wall Street Journal Best Selling Author

JON SPOELSTRA

Is it fair
to have an unfair advantage?

GET YOUR IDEAS APPROVED is not a book about negotiations.

With negotiations, there's often give-and-take. There are compromises. There's settling on a middle ground.

None of those are applicable in this book.

This book is about getting *your idea* approved by *your boss*; about getting your idea approved the way *you* want to make it work.

This book is the proven blueprint on how to get the approval you need and want without taking a risk.

It really is your *unfair advantage* in getting your boss to approve whatever you want to initiate.

So, is it unfair to use an unfair advantage to get an approval from your boss? Of course not. In this case, an unfair advantage is a fair advantage. *Your* advantage.

Here it is, your advantage. Go ahead, use it, run with it. You and your boss will be delighted that you did.

Witnesses
to Approvals

"I worked with Jon at two places, and it was stunning how he'd get things approved when most would have bet the ranch against him."

Howie Nuchow
Co-Head, CAA Sports

"I just thought Jon's ideas just came to him. Like poof! Now I understand this magical guru of ideas actually had an idea plan, committed to practice and then a stalwart defense of that idea."

Buffy Filippell
Founder, Teamwork Online

"I am fortunate to have started my career in sports working and learning from Jon. As he has done again and again, Jon gets approvals from difficult ideas that make a difference."

Scott O'Neil
CEO, Philadephia 76ers

"I have had the good fortune to work with some of the best and brightest minds in the sports and entertainment business. By far, the brightest mind, the most entrepreneurial leader and thinker is Jon. He is brilliant at ideas, but even better at converting them into reality."

Tim Leiwicke
CEO, Oak View Group
(former CEO of Staples Center & LA Kings)

"Jon presented some out-of-the-box ideas during my time as owner of the Portland Trail Blazers. It got to the point where even if the idea was far-out, I'd sit back and just enjoy watching how he got me to say yes. In some respects, it wasn't fair."

Larry Weinberg
former owner of the Portland Trail Blazers

"Jon's most exceptional skill is he got things—*breakthrough* things–approved that most guys wouldn't even try. And, he got those things approved with no bloodshed, no shouting, no arm twisting."

Steve DeLay
owner, Macon Bacon

"Jon has seldom heard 'no'....his conviction for what he believes in can overwhelm you.

When he has heard no, few have been better in turning a no into an approval."

Brett Yormark
Co-CEO of RocNation Unified

"I remember seeing many of the creative ideas Jon brought to life over the years. I often wondered first, 'How did he think of that?.' Then second, 'How the heck did he ever get that approved?' Now I know. I wish I'd had this info 40 years ago.

Steve Patterson
President, Pro Sports Consulting

"Jon Spoelstra was a mentor for me in my early sports career. His invocations set the pace for the entire sports world—he got new exciting things approved! And from those formative days, Jon continued to be a true trail blazer and still is today, as evidenced by the thinking in this book.

Tod Leiwicke
CEO, NHL Seattle

"This is like a master magician showing you step-by-step how to do his most famous magic trick, but this is better—you learn the secret on how to get your boss to approve whatever you want to do.

Joe Sugarman
Chairman, BluBlocker Sunglasses

"Jon had this crazy idea, and I personally saw him get an impossible approval from a gauntlet of bosses. We were all amazed."

Mike Nealy
CEO, Global Events Group

"I wish I had known about The Outrageous Approval Tool decades ago. It would have been a godsend in some difficult jobs I've had in the past."

Darrell Rutter
CEO, TMG, Inc.

Table of
Contents

1

The Outrageous Approval Tool

There's one question asked of me more than any other during the Q&A at any one of my speeches.

"What *one thing* is most responsible for your successes?"

Yes, I have had some marketing successes, and I've written about those successes in *Marketing Outrageously, Marketing Outrageously Redux* and *Ice to the Eskimos.*

This book is about the one thing most responsible for my successes: How I have been able to get my bosses to approve anything and everything I wanted to initiate.

My approval percentage is 100%. That includes the really wacky stuff.

I got bosses of all types to approve things. I'm talking about tough bosses, cunning bosses, brilliant bosses, bosses who hated me, bosses who didn't want to approve anything I did, bosses that loved me, government bosses and even wonderful bosses.

THE FIRST TIME

The first time I got my boss to approve something important that I wanted to initiate, I didn't think that it was a career enhancer.

No, my thoughts weren't that lofty; I was just pleased that I had the go-sign to bring my idea to life.

It wasn't until a year or so later that I realized I used a tool—yes, an actual *tool*—that I could use as frequently as I wanted to get my boss(es) to approve anything I wanted to do.

I'm not talking about trivial stuff to get approved. I'm talking about ideas that could appear risky—some may even say *ridiculously* dangerous to a career.

I'm not sure of the danger, but I'll grant you that these ideas were *different*. Being different by itself could scare off some folks from even *thinking* about asking the boss for approval unless they had what I now call **The Outrageous Approval Tool**. Having that Tool is a game-changer.

Throughout my career, I went back to use The Outrageous Approval Tool and it *never* failed me. You see, some things in life are just not fair, and using The Outrageous Approval Tool is not fair to your boss. You'll get the approval every time. You just have to use it.

2

The most important yardstick

Picture this: You're standing with me at the middle of a basketball court. I put a basketball in your hand.

I ask you to heave that basketball at one of the baskets—all 47 feet away—and have the ball go through the hoop.

"Go ahead, try to make it," I say, nodding to one of the hoops.

You reach back and throw the ball like you would a football. The bookmakers in Las Vegas would say that the odds would be 100-to-1 that you'd miss. So, let's follow the odds and say you miss.

"Take another shot," I say and flip you another basketball.

You miss again.

We repeat this five times. All misses.

After this demonstration of futility, I ask you, "Which is more difficult? Making a shot from half-court or taking a crazy idea and getting it approved by your boss?"

Without hesitation, you might say getting approval from the boss for a crazy idea is far more difficult—maybe even impossible—than a half-court shot.

You might say, "It's not a big deal if I miss a shot from half-court. We were just having fun. Pitching my boss on an idea isn't fun. And, it could have consequences. And besides, with a half-court shot I could get lucky."

I grant you that right now, it may seem a lot *scarier* pitching your boss a new idea. However, let's first look at what the odds are and then take a peek at the degree of scariness.

1. The odds of making a half-court shot are 100-to-1.

2. The odds of getting your boss to approve your ideas will be 1-to-1. 1-to-1 means you'll get your idea approved every time you pitch an important idea to your boss. *"Hah,"* you scoff, "easy for you to say—you don't know my boss." You're right, I don't know your boss nor what your idea is. But for a few moments, suspend your disbelief and assume that the 1-to-1 was true if you used The Outrageous Approval Tool. Imagine your *level of confidence* in presenting an idea to your boss *knowing* that you'll get it approved. Your confidence would never have been greater. You'll find that using The Outrageous Approval Tool will bring you unbridled confidence.

If the 1-to-1 odds are indeed accurate, we can probably remove 'scare' out of the equation. After all, how scary is it to get your ideas approved all the time? And, if we wanted to talk about consequences, we can talk about *good* consequences.

THE MOST IMPORTANT YARDSTICK

The most important yardstick in getting an approval is not your boss; it is *you*. So, let's look first at some attributes that may describe you:

1. **Crazy ideas or semi-crazy ideas are not uncommon to you**. Upon first being heard,

a real breakthrough idea sounds crazy. Most folks laugh or cringe when they first hear the idea. Some even fall down laughing. Heck, if people didn't think one of my ideas was crazy, I start to feel the idea doesn't have merit as a breakthrough idea. You probably have a few of these types of ideas, maybe a lot more than a few. That's good. Crazy ideas are good; crazy ideas are often breakthrough ideas.

2. **You have a hunger to control your destiny**. Because you're reading this book, I think you want to improve what you do for a living today. Most often, that means improving the part of your job in your company or organization that impedes your personal growth. And, most likely, that means you need to get approval from your boss for those things you want to dramatically (or even radically) improve. Getting to do what you want is indeed controlling your destiny.

3. **You're willing to take chances if it's a semi sure-thing**. If you're satisfied to follow the follower where you work, then this book probably isn't for you. If you're like me, you're at least willing to take chances as long as it looks like a semi sure-thing. If

that's the case, The Outrageous Approval
Tool is for you. It may seem outrageous, but
it's not dangerous.

For you to even consider using The Outrageous
Approval Tool, I would bet that at least two of the following points are essential to you. You'll notice that
education, age, experience, height-weight-gender, IQ,
the color of your hair, etc. were not on the list of attributes. What's important here is that you identify with at
least two of the three attributes above.

Let's say you have attribute #2, but not #1 and #3.
Sorry, your chances of getting an idea approved by your
boss are not good. In this case, you've got to have ideas
and a willingness to take a chance.

What if you have attribute #3, but no ideas and no
hunger? Not bad. If you could partner with somebody
who has the idea—and you're will to take the
chance—you've got a good chance your idea approved.

One attribute is not enough. If you have only one
attribute, you could partner up with somebody to give
you the second and/or third attribute. If you've got all
three, that's terrific!

What you need—one way or the other—is two out of
the three attributes. If you got them, and you use The
Outrageous Approval Tool, you'll get your ideas
approved by your boss.

You have at least two of three: ideas, hunger, verve.
Pick any two.

WHERE IT WILL WORK

I spent most of my adult life working in the business side of professional sports. Here's part of my resume:

Buffalo Braves: VP-Marketing

Portland Trail Blazers: Senior VP & GM

Denver Nuggets: President & GM

New Jersey Nets: President & COO

Mandalay Baseball: Pres. & Managing Director

Savannah Bananas: Minority Owner

Macon Bacon: Co-Owner

In my marketing books, I wrote about some tactics and strategies that worked for me and for others outside the world of sports. The books were sort of a compendium of *thinking different* in marketing.

This book, however, is an autobiography of how I got things approved. I only cover what has worked for me. This is my memoir of how I got things, mostly wildly different things, approved.

The question then could be: does it work in other industries than pro sports? Does it work with different bosses?

The strategies that I used to get approvals are timeless;

they will work whether I used them years ago or use them years from now.

The fundamentals of getting something approved by your boss are the same as when I went for approvals from my bosses. Sure, the ideas that you want to get approved are different, but the fundamentals are exactly the same.

When you finish the book, I think you'll come to the same conclusion as this: It doesn't make much difference what the ideas are or who the bosses are or which industry you're in. The Outrageous Approval Tool will work at any company or organization in any field.

3

When I first found The Tool

I was 37 years old when I discovered The Outrageous Approval Tool and how to use it.

It was 1979, and I had just joined the Portland Trail Blazers, a team in the National Basketball Association.

At that time, things were immensely different in the NBA. For instance, I was the Blazers' tenth front-office employee; today a typical NBA team will have a front office of 150 or more employees.

The team used to travel with about 15 people (12 players, two coaches, one trainer and one radio play-by-play announcer). Today, the traveling party for a team is closer to 38 with 15 players, one head coach, at least 5 assistant coaches, 2-4 trainers, 2 strength coaches, 1-2 equipment managers, one security chief, and one chef and 6-8 radio and TV announcers and producers.

The player salaries were, of course, vastly different. A high-priced player back in 1979 might make $200,000 a season. That was a tidy sum back then, but doesn't compare to the possible *$40+ million per season* today.

Yes, the dollars were vastly different, but there was at

least one crucial thing that is the same today as back then; you had to get things approved by a boss or bosses. Let me repeat: The one thing that is the same from era to era or industry to industry is you have to get big ideas approved by a boss.

MY FIRST REAL TEST

Here's the scenario I entered in 1979. The Blazers had won the NBA championship just two years before. Strangely, their revenue from local TV and radio went down a bit after the Championship. The owner, Larry Weinberg, hired me as a one-day consultant to get my thoughts on the matter. I threw out a bunch of ideas—stuff I thought I'd like to *try*, but no sports team had ever done so at that time. He liked my enthusiasm and offered me the job of Vice President of Marketing of the Portland Trail Blazers.

There was one hitch. I had to present any new ideas to the president of the team. The president, however, firmly believed 'if it ain't broken, don't fix it.' In case I didn't understand that phrase, he voiced it repeatedly and often to me.

Here's the idea I was going to propose: I wanted to do something different with our radio broadcasts. At the time, the Blazers received a 'rights fee' from a local radio station allowing the station to broadcast the games exclusively. The station paid all costs, including announcer, airtime, engineering, travel, etc. The station sold commercial time, and after paying the Blazers and all the expenses, they kept whatever profit was left. That's the way every NBA team did it at the time.

Radio rights fees were not big dollar items for a team. Even though the Blazers rights fee was the third-best in the entire NBA, it was only $25,000 a season.

I wanted the Portland Trail Blazers to risk that $25,000, plus spend tens of thousands of dollars to bring radio "in-house."

"In-house" wasn't wording that was used by sports teams in those days, but here's what it meant: the games would still be broadcast on the radio station, but we would get no rights fee. The only thing the station would do was provide the signal to broadcast the games. The Blazers would be responsible for the production of the games as well as selling sponsorships. We would pay all the costs, including the salary of the play-by-play announcer, his travel expenses, engineering costs, station airtime costs, my salary, the salary of my assistant and anything else related to the broadcasts.

The station would do this because it would have nighttime 'public service' programming at absolutely no cost and no risk.

We would do this because I would make the case that the Blazers could make a lot more than $25,000 from its radio broadcasts by bringing it in-house and with me selling sponsorships.

All I had to do was present the idea to a guy who firmly believed if it ain't broken, don't fix it. In other words, just take the $25,000 and bank it.

It didn't take too much for me to imagine how a meeting with my 'if-it-ain't-broken boss' would go:

Me

"Hey, I've got a new idea. We could make a lot more money with our radio broadcasts." (I would then briefly explain the idea of bringing radio in-house.)

Boss

"Which teams in the NBA have done this?"

Me

"None that I know of."

Boss

"Which pro team in sports has done this?"

Me

"None that I know of."

Boss

"If nobody else has done it, there's probably a reason. It won't work. Why would we risk our $25,000 doing something that nobody has done before, and it probably wouldn't work anyway?"

Me

"Because we could make a lot more than $25,000."

Boss

"You need to prove this to me before we make a decision to do it or not."

The boss would then offer me some encouragement.

Boss

"You know, you should be thinking about something more practical. Instead of that radio idea, you could sell an ad on the back of the ticket envelopes. Probably get a couple thousand bucks for it. Would you please close the door on your way out of my office?" (It was only a couple of years later that he mechanized the closure of his office door. With the push of a button at his desk, his office door would swing closed, sometimes quickly. If you didn't move fast enough, it would indeed hit you on the ass as you walked out.)

I envisioned that scenario as entirely plausible.

PROVE IT TO ME

Proving it was not going to be a casual endeavor. I would need to prepare as I had never before.

I'm not talking about a cramming session before a final exam like in college, where I'd pop some No-Doz to try to stop my eyes from glazing over the pages of a textbook. Nope, I'm talking about something far more intense.

Here's how intense: Suppose I was defending myself in front of the Supreme Court where, if I win, I walk away scot-free. If I lost, I'd rot in prison for the rest of my life.

Rot in prison? How thoroughly would I prepare to avoid that? How intensely would *you* prepare if you were facing the chance of rotting in some maximum-security prison? No country club incarceration for you.

Am I over-dramatizing? Some would think so. But, while I would not be defending my life or my freedom in front of the Supreme Court, I would be defending *my career* in front of *my* Supreme Court.

MY SUPREME COURT

Labeling my boss as the Supreme Court was not hyperbole. My boss was, indeed, *my* Supreme Court. If he didn't approve what I wanted to do, I would have been relegated to being a lifetime witness to 'if it ain't broken, don't fix it.' My boss was *my* judge and *my* jury, and perhaps *my* executioner, simple as that.

I had a choice. I could muster up just enough effort to wing it and hope for the best; or, I could prepare more seriously than any preparation I had ever done in my life to convince a staunch naysayer to let me run with my idea, crazy as it may be.

I chose to prepare as if my life (career) depended on it.

Who is the Justice on your Supreme Court?

4
The Starting Line

There were some severe handicaps in my preparation to bring radio in-house:

1. **I had no experience in radio sales**. I didn't know how radio stations worked; I wasn't even acquainted with a radio salesperson where I could get an insider perspective. Heck, I had never been inside a radio station in my life. The only experience I had with radio was watching the sitcom *WKRP* on television and listening to the radio while I drove my car.

WKRP is about all I knew of what a radio station was.

2. **There were no public resources I could use to help me prepare.** In those days, there was no YouTube, no Google, no Internet. How in the world did we find out *anything* in those days?

3. **There was nobody in Portland I could bounce a few ideas off of**. I had just moved to Portland, Oregon and didn't know anybody. This was going to be a solo effort.

However, there were two big plusses:

a. **I had sold sports sponsorships**. It's not like I was an aeronautical engineer leaping with my slide rule into sponsorship sales. I had sold sponsorships before, it just wasn't with radio included.

b. **I had experience in writing sponsorship proposals**. These were mostly individualized proposals. This experience was a great benefit because I was used to writing proposals where the objective was to get the reader to approve what was proposed.

WHERE TO START?

Good ideas often get spiked at the beginning. The kill-shot to these ideas is often the boss's *first* objection. And, if the first objection didn't do the job, the second objection would finish the idea off.

In the scenario I imagined with my boss, it was this simple objection: "Which teams in the NBA have done this?" that could have derailed me. Without significant preparation, I probably would have stumbled a bit in answering that question. Stumbling, by the way, almost always means on-the-spot death of the idea.

Yes, this would take some planning.

I decided that my presentation to get the approval of bringing radio in-house would have two components:

1. The Written Proposal. This document would be the complete outline and summary of my "Radio In-House" idea. I would sequence the pages to exactly how I would make the verbal presentation. This written proposal would be like a 'leave behind' piece that we used in sponsorship sales pitches.

GET YOUR HANDS OFF!

My written proposal would be visible—in my hands—at the meeting. At no time during the verbal presentation, however, would I allow my boss to review the written portion, even if he asked. If he did ask, I'd tell him, "You can have this (written proposal) later, but let's just discuss the idea now." I felt that if I handed my boss the written proposal and he skimmed it while I talked, I should start digging a grave for that idea. The idea would be dead the moment I handed over the written proposal, slowly dying while I was talking.

The primary purpose of the written proposal was to organize *my arguments in the proper sequence and wording.* It was to become, in essence, my script.

A secondary purpose was as a visual prop connoting *credibility.* As a prop, it would signify to my boss that this was far more serious than just a conversation that started with, "Hey, I've got an idea I would like to discuss with you…" The written proposal showed that I had done some serious thinking about the idea and that I was serious enough to put it all in writing.

The written proposal was also a tool for any *hidden* decision-makers. We often don't know who the boss might discuss the idea with. I wouldn't want my boss to be the one to represent my idea just on his own to any hidden decision-makers. I want my thoroughly prepared proposal in my boss's hands as a possible reference tool to some essential points. Or, if my boss handed the written proposal to someone else and said, "Tell me what you think," I wanted it to be my words doing the convincing.

One word of warning: While the written proposal wouldn't be the closer, it could be the murderer of the idea the boss was ready to approve if it's poorly written, littered with typos and filled with hyperbole.

As important as the written proposal was for my preparation, I didn't fool myself into thinking that the written proposal would be the deciding factor in convincing my boss to approve my idea. That would be the job of Point #2, **The Verbal Presentation**.

2. The Verbal Presentation. No matter how well-done the written proposal may be, it was up to me in the verbal presentation to get the approval. I would not be winging this; my verbal pitch would follow the path of the written proposal.

Now all I had to do was assemble the parts and then practice, practice, practice my pitch.

Allen Iverson's opinion of practice was different than mine.

5

Insanely serious prep time

You're preparing to get the idea *accepted*. Your primary weapon is the depth and intensity of your preparation.

You're preparing to get the idea accepted.

The written part of the preparation shouldn't be in tedious volumes. Think in terms of a written Executive Summary that will be six or seven pages. 10-11 pages top.

Wait a minute! Everybody knows preparation for the Supreme Court could take *thousands* of pages, maybe *tens of thousands of pages* of material. What's this six or seven-page stuff?

Well, you're going to work like it is indeed thousands of pages, but you're going to distill it down to six or seven pages.

The written preparation (or 'Executive Summary') should have five parts:

PART 1: FOREWORD
_____

Consider the Foreword as a 'State of the Nation' in the

area of the organization where the new idea would be applied.

With my 'radio in-house' idea, I gave a very straightforward view of the situation at the time. It would have included the following facts:

a. **Fact:** The Blazers received $25,000 a year from a radio station.

b. **Fact:** That fee was third-best in the NBA.

c. **Fact:** No other team had radio in-house.

d. **Statement:** I propose that the Blazers could make much more income from its radio broadcasts. I would not elaborate on this statement here; in the next section, I would elaborate on why and how the Blazers could make a lot more money from their radio broadcasts.

I would not sugarcoat anything here, nor would I slant the facts. The Foreword has to be an unemotional and accurate representation of the situation.

If the Foreword is not accurate, or if there's a bunch of hype language, then you could be challenged by your boss right from the get-go. If the opening assessment is tainted, then the solution (your idea) will be considered tainted.

The Foreword is a vital point in establishing your credibility in recognizing the opportunity. The length could vary from one to two pages.

PART 2: CONCEPT

The Concept is a concise written statement of what the idea is. In the case of bringing radio in-house, I would clearly state the pertinent details:

We have the opportunity to bring radio in-house. By bringing radio in-house, we could dramatically increase our radio income.

Bringing our radio broadcasts in-house would mean we would be responsible for selling all of the commercial time. We would also be responsible for all of its expenses. There would be no cost for the air-time at the radio station.

We would receive all the commercial time in the play-by-play portion of each broadcast and keep 100% of the proceeds. The radio station would receive 50% of the commercial time in the pre-game and post-game shows and would keep the proceeds of whatever they sold.

Jon Spoelstra, the Blazers VP-Marketing, would be selling the commercial time. Bill Schonely would continue as the Blazers play-by-play announcer.

Jon's assistant would do the billing, trafficking of commercials, etc.

We would not be receiving the $25,000 rights fee from the radio station. However, our profit from our radio broadcasts should exceed $100,000.

The Concept section should be one page with the possibility of extending into a partial second page.

As with the Foreword, hyperbole should not be used here. In the verbal presentation, you could use emotion and some hyperbole, but the written document has to be unemotional and factual. Using hype and a bunch of exclamation points in the written proposal could impair my credibility.

PART 3: RATIONALE

The Rationale is the section where you state your primary arguments. Why should the Portland Trail Blazers initiate this idea of bringing radio in-house? What's in it for the team? In this case—as it often is—is money.

How much money?

I felt that we could easily increase the profit from the radio broadcasts of our games by 800%. That may sound stark raving crazy, and a way-over-the-top projection and uber-hyped, but I did have experience in selling sports sponsorships, and I felt that the radio station had *underpriced* the Blazers inventory they had sold. They didn't underprice it intentionally. They just sold the way they usually sold—radio spots at a highly negotiated price.

By bringing radio in-house, we had a lot more enhancements we could add that would make the radio sponsorship more valuable to a business. We wouldn't just be selling 60-second radio commercials that would air in the games; we would be selling *sponsorships that included much more.*

One of the enhancements we had was choice season tickets. The Blazers had won the NBA Championship in 1977 and had sold every ticket to every game since then. A Blazers radio sponsor with the radio station used to receive tickets to a few games. By buying a radio sponsorship from us, the sponsor company would get tickets to *every* game.

And, a *reserved* parking spot in the players' lot.

And a player appearance at their business.

And, a Blazers promotion explicitly created for each radio sponsor.

We could clearly sell the sponsorships for a lot more money than the radio station could. By selling *just one* of our radio sponsorship packages I had created, we would cover all of our expenses and equal the $25,000 we received from the radio station in a rights fee deal.

In this section, I would elaborate on the details: How much is the new revenue; how much is it going to cost; what's the net income; how long will it take before the revenue rolls in? I did a simple cash flow to cover all of that.

The Rationale section could take about two pages. (In one other instance, it took me over 20 pages to thoroughly explain the value of the idea, but this was for a complicated idea that required an investment of millions of dollars, not just $25,000.)

PART 4: PROBLEMS (QUESTIONS & OBJECTIONS & OTHER PHENOMENA)

The Problems section often needs to be the most convincing part of the proposal.

This section is all about the questions, objections and potential problems that the boss will have.

This is more than just anticipating any cursory objections you would expect to encounter in trying to sell the idea. You must take one step further; you need to deduce the questions/problems/objections that you would *not* expect.

Once you've done that to an exhaustive degree, you need to create compelling answers to those questions/problems/objections. No shortcuts can be taken here: you've got to come up with every possible question/problem/objection *before* the boss does, and have compelling answers *in writing*.

Trust me, there's no way you would skate through the oral presentation without facing some severe objections, including at least one death-spiral question. After all, bosses are experts when it comes to objections.

Whenever I did this exercise with staff members, we spent *hours* coming up with convincing answers to 'boss-like' questions. The boss-like questions can be legit questions, and other questions that can be downright nasty. We put the questions we thought most important into our written preparation, and we were now fully prepared to answer even the most loathsome shoot-from-the-hip questions.

Thinking of objections days before the boss does is a vital step in preparing how to overcome those objections. You certainly don't want to answer a tough question when the first time you hear it from the mouth of your boss.

You're preparing yourself to win. How you handle these objections in front of your Supreme Court is the determining factor whether you win or lose.

To add a dimension to my boss's questions, I usually would conjure up a "Guest Questioner" in my preparation. My favorite Guest Questioner was the owner of the Blazers at the time of my radio in-house idea, Larry Weinberg. He was the best questioner I've ever faced. I learned that when he hired me as a one-day consultant. He came up with the types of questions I had never experienced before. Some were seemingly off-the-wall, but strangely always became pertinent to the subject. From that one-day experience, I always used the personification of Larry as my Guest Questioner. If you have a boss like that or one from your past who was a great questioner, then bring that boss along as an imaginary Guest Questioner.

The Problems section might be the longest in the written proposal. Take several pages in this area if need be.

PART 5: SUMMARY

By now, you most likely will have won your case, but

you might not have received the formal approval. This Summary section is a *Call for Approval* and has a specific timetable for approval and implementation.

It could look something like this: The most advantageous time to initiate this idea would be _____ (time of the year). To get geared up, we would need approvals by _____ (specific date).

The Summary (last) section could be done in one or two paragraphs.

ONE WORD OF CAUTION

One word of warning about the written document: Watch the hype! Do not use ALL CAPS or exclamation points!!!! **Don't use a lot of BOLDING!!!**

Go through the document and look at every adjective, adverb, and wildly assertive sentence. Eliminate those that you find. A proposal that's hyped too strongly will lose its credibility.

You can use hype, but not in this document. It's easier to use hype and emotion during the oral presentation without losing credibility. In the oral presentation, you are *talking;* it won't be examined and re-examined like a written document.

6

The Pitch

When I was a young salesperson, I easily had stage fright when pitching an idea to a person who I considered a 'big shot.'

The first company I worked for was small and didn't offer any training, so I learned using the trial-and-error method or the trial-and-error-error-error method.

I seemed to do okay with the normal business people I would call on, but when I had to present to a vice president (or God forbid, the president or owner of a company), I was not persuasive at all. As inexperienced as I was, I did realize I had to do something about it.

Sure, I bought plenty of paperback books that featured selling. I still have some of these in my home library. I might request these books be buried with me:

The Magic of Believing is my all-time favorite, and it also became my son's favorite. He believed he could win championships in the NBA.

To overcome the fear of presenting to big-shots, I spent an excessive amount of time practicing my pitch, particularly in handling objections. To flawlessly handle objections, I, of course, had to anticipate them first.

In one case, I took the practice to an extreme. I was selling for a company that sold to health and beauty companies like Proctor & Gamble, Gillette, Helene Curtis, Johnson & Johnson, etc. One company we could not get a contract with was Alberto-Culver. The owner of the company I worked for couldn't get a contract with Alberto-Culver; the president of the company I worked for couldn't get it done; I tried for a year and also couldn't get it done. In that year of calling on different Alberto-Culver executives and failing, I heard anecdotes about the owner and founder, Leonard Lavin. Lavin was reputed to be tough—really tough. Legend had it he enjoyed seeing presenters crumble before his very eyes during intense meetings. And, Lavin made *all* the decisions that mattered and almost all the decisions that didn't matter.

If an order from Alberto-Culver were ever possible, I would have to go into the lion's den and risk crumbling before Leonard Lavin's very eyes, then getting chewed up and spit out.

My only chance, I thought, to not crumbling would be extreme preparation.

I had heard that Lavin would interrupt a presentation with loud and sometimes profane objections that could quickly kill a few thousand of the presenter's brain cells. So, I had to practice rude and profane interruptions, take the blast of scorching heat and somehow get back on track. I practiced my pitch forward and backward. I worked on every crazy objection that Lavin could hurl at me.

I lassoed a friend of mine to play the part of Leonard Lavin. My buddy would listen to my pitch, and then at different times during the pitch, he would rudely—loudly and profanely—interrupt me with a question. I had prepared a catalog of questions, many of them crazy, that my buddy could use or he could make up his own. After a week, I was ready.

I got the meeting with Leonard Lavin (that's another story in itself).

When I walked into the lion's den, I surprisingly didn't feel nervous. The only thing I carried in with me was a spiral-bound booklet, my written proposal. There was no flip-flop presentation kit, no big salesman's briefcase, no props, nothing but me and my spiral-bound booklet. I considered this to be a professional meeting between two executives, albeit one was highly junior and the other was a grizzled senior.

Leonard Lavin sure doesn't look that tough in this exec photo. Don't be fooled.

About one minute into my pitch, Lavin yelled an objection. Under normal circumstances, that would have floored me; just scrape me up and deposit me outside.

I listened to his rant, and amazingly, kept my composure and answered his objection. I think he was more surprised at my composure than I was.

Another two minutes into my pitch, Lavin fired another full-blast objection complete with spittle flying. I didn't crumble.

A minute later, he asked if that was the written offer in my hand. I said yes. He said he wanted to look at it. I told him that I would give it to him after we discussed my proposal.

About fifteen minutes later, he told me I had a deal. We shook hands.

He then took the written proposal and briefly leafed through it. We shook hands again. He told me to coordinate the deal with specific employees he named.

I walked out of the lion's den not only alive but with a sale and a lifetime experience wrapped up in one twenty-minute segment.

I never saw Lavin again, but I did see in the *Wall Street Journal* that he died in 2017 at the ripe old age of 97. He had become a noted philanthropist and thoroughbred breeder. I've often thought of that experience and the profound effect it had on me, particularly in the necessity of outrageous preparation.

THE LEONARD LAVIN STYLE OF PREP

Getting approval from my boss to bring radio in-house was a big deal for me. A really big deal. I had turned down a great opportunity with another company and had moved my family to Portland, Oregon. If I didn't get the approval to bring radio in-house, my future would be relegated to selling ad space on the back of ticket envelopes. My career would be squishing around in the mud.

So I prepared Leonard Lavin style. I didn't have a buddy in Portland to play the Leonard Lavin role, but I improvised playing both parts.

My boss at the Blazers wasn't nearly as explosive as Lavin, but he was indeed formidable. However, I think I muted him right from the get-go with my preparation.

The only mildly tense portion of the pitch was when he asked, "Why in the world do you think a radio station would give you the air time to broadcast the games for *free*? They're not stupid."

I said, "Good question, I've outlined the reason on page 6 (pointing to the cover my spiral-bound proposal) which I'll give to you later, but the reason is…"

(I had learned, by the way, that the Blazers had terrific radio ratings for their radio broadcasts. Their ratings at night were greater than morning drive ratings on any station in town. I felt that whichever radio station we went with would have a fabulous competitive advantage in the Portland market because that station would have blockbuster ratings at night with the Blazers. Those huge ratings could easily spill over to boost the station's morning drive ratings, which is where the stations made most of their revenue.)

My answer seemed to take the wind out of my boss' sails. The next couple of questions were just asked more for the sake of asking, something to fill space.

That same day my boss called me to his office.

He told me to go ahead with bringing radio in-house.

He didn't tell me to close the door on my way out of his office.

THE RESULTS

Getting your idea approved by your boss is a three-step process.

The first step is the insanely severe preparation.

The second step is getting the approval.

The third step is delivering on what you proposed.

This third step in bringing radio in-house turned out to be a massive step. Instead of earning the $100,000 I had projected, which was 400% more than the right's fee from the radio station the year before, our profit soared to almost $900,000.

That's right. $900,000! (exclamation point intended).

The final profit results even surprised me. I knew that earning $100,000 was going to be relatively easy. In my mind, I expected we would earn about $500,000, but I didn't use that number in the presentation because I thought it might appear too good to be possible.

The $900,000 was a shot heard 'round the NBA because it was greater profit from radio than the rest of the NBA combined!

Strange things happened after that. For instance, the

Indiana Pacers wanted to bring radio in-house and get the financial rewards like the Blazers were getting. They were so serious that they were willing to trade their starting point guard for me to come to Indianapolis to show them how to do it. You can check out the full story on YouTube:

If you want to watch, go to YouTube and type in the search bar the following: Craziest NBA Trade and press enter.

Two years after we brought radio in-house, our agreement with the TV station that telecast our games was expiring. Even though the TV rights fee was a lot higher at $200,000 per season, the obvious move for the Blazers would be to bring TV telecasts in-house.

Not so. My boss was close friends with the General Manager at the TV station. My boss said we should do some form of a partnership. He outlined what he thought a fair deal would be. I thought that would work terrifically for the TV station, but only marginally beneficial for the Blazers.

So, it was back to using The Outrageous Approval Tool. I did the full process: the seven-page proposal, the thorough preparation, even a modified Leonard Lavin rehearsal of the pitch. I made the pitch to both the owner of the Blazers and my boss.

I waited for this question to be asked by my boss, "Don't you think it would be better if we partnered up with the TV station than taking this bigger risk on our own?"

It was almost as if I had scripted that question for my boss. Of course, I had! My answer was also scripted, "No. As you'll see on page 6, we fare a lot better—it isn't even close—by *not* partnering with the TV station, but by bringing television in-house just like we did with radio."

There are some things in life that are plumb not fair. This was one of them.

We brought the TV telecasts in-house. Our profit increased ten-fold from $200,000 to over $2,000,000.

7

When to open the toolbox

When I come up with a big idea that would need the approval of my boss or even the Board of Directors, my first question to myself is

How important is this idea?

If it's imperative—and I'll give you a few more examples later on in this book—then I first have to commit *myself* to take the necessary time to make the proper outrageous preparation.

There have been times when, alas, I have been tempted to short-cut the approval process. After all, the outrageous preparation always took mountains of time. But then I'd ask myself a variation of the first question:

How badly do I want to do this idea?

If breathing life into an idea that was genuinely compelling to me, I would not take the chance of *not* doing the outrageous preparation. Even though my bosses knew what I could do, and knew that I would deliver on what I said I would, I didn't want to risk getting an idea I really wanted to do get blown out of the water by a single crazed question/objection. For example, if I presented an idea to my Supreme Court that I was excited about in a *What-do-you-think* manner, and it got unmercifully squashed, it would be almost impossible to bring it to life.

With most significant ideas—like the idea of bringing radio in-house—I would have only *one shot* in front of my Supreme Court. I couldn't allow myself to lose the decision because of a *lack of preparation*. How utterly awful would that be? If the idea was worthy to me, I would *prepare for that meeting as if my life depended on it.*

HOW WOULD *YOU* PREPARE IF *YOUR* LIFE DEPENDED ON IT?

Life depending on it? Yeah, yeah, I know I'm over-dramatizing again. Or am I? Over the years, my career has been essential to me. It has provided for my family and me generously, that's a real plus. And, my career has given me the freedom to do what I want to do. That makes every day a lot more fun and fulfilling. My life—as I have enjoyed it—was dependent on how serious I would prepare to get to do the things I wanted to do the way I wanted to do them.

So, before I went to my boss to get permission on something, I would ask myself those two questions:

1. How important is this idea to me?

2. How badly do I want to do this idea?

Those two questions sound very me-centric. Well, they are. If it's a great idea and it's approved, the company certainly benefits, along with me. Conversely, if you're not enthusiastic about the idea and it's not important to you, why go through the depths of preparation?

Those two questions could also sound like the same question, just stated two different ways. If they are similar, so what? I would ask those two questions to myself anyway. If my answer was "so-so" or something like that, I might take the risk and just talk about it with my boss with no massive preparation. If my boss gave permission, terrific; if my boss said 'no way,' that was okay too.

However, if my answer to my first question—how important is this idea—was 'a lot' or something like that, I wouldn't risk even mentioning the idea to my boss. I didn't want to risk a premature 'no.' By getting the answer 'a lot,' I knew I had to roll up my sleeves and prepare The Outrageous Approval Tool.

8

No one-hit wonders

In 1969 Norman Greenbaum had his only hit as a solo recording artist, "Spirit in the Sky." Remember the lyrics?

> When I die and they lay me to rest
> Gonna go to the place that's the best
> When I lay me down to die
> Goin' up to the spirit in the sky
> Goin' up to the spirit in the sky
> That's where I'm gonna go when I die

There have been a lot more one-hit wonders. Here's just a few:

- Bobby Day with "Rockin' Robin" (1958)

- Bruce Channel with "Hey! Baby!" (1961)

- The Surfaris with "Wipe Out" (1963)

- The Archies with "Sugar, Sugar" (1969)

- King Harvest with "Dancing in the Moonlight" (1972)

A skeptic might think that I just got lucky with my first shot of using The Outrageous Approval Tool. A skeptic might think my name could be an addition to the list of one-hit wonders.

Not so. Once I used The Outrageous Approval Tool, I found myself using it again and again. Once you use The Outrageous Approval Tool, you'll experience the same thing. By doing so, you are creating your destiny, approval by approval.

My experience has been that once you use The Outrageous Approval Tool that it becomes lodged somewhere in a small, narrow space of your brain, lingers there until it sneaks back to the surface, emerging to your consciousness when you least expect it. You then get the feeling that it's time to initiate something new, something that's big enough that you'll need to get your boss's approval. Slowly you start assembling the thoughts and pieces that you'll need to clarify the idea, and then it picks up momentum, and it's off to the races.

If you'd like to see how The Outrageous Approval Tool would re-emerge with different ideas, I've included six Case Studies where I went all-in to get an idea approved.

With these real-life examples, you'll see how off-the-wall ideas became a reality by using The Outrageous Approval Tool.

CASE STUDY #1: LET'S RENT OUR OWN SATELLITE!

When we brought radio in-house, we built a 41-station network. Our Blazers broadcasts reached every nook and cranny in Oregon, southwest Washington, and the tip of northern California. The stations received the feed by an enhanced telephone connection via AT&T. Everything was fine for a couple of years, and then AT&T wanted to raise the rates ten-fold for our enhanced telephone lines.

We looked for alternative ways of sending our broadcasts. Nothing. After all, AT&T had a monopoly back then.

"How about satellite?" one of our staffers asked. Satellite transmissions were in the early stages, and only big companies like the national TV networks were going up in the sky.

We inquired anyway. In those days, you could not rent a satellite by the hour or even by the month. You could only rent a satellite transponder *by the year*. Twenty-four hours a day multiplied by 365 days a year would be 8,760 hours of transmissions per year. We only needed a sliver of that time—about 246 hours for the entire season (82 game broadcasts by 3 hours).

To go with satellite transmission, we would have to

buy an uplink (a big piece of equipment which beamed the broadcasts to the satellite). Additionally, we would have to purchase downlinks for all of our stations (many stations didn't have one at that time). These items would be expensive. We did the math anyway.

Surprisingly, the price tag for everything came in *lower* than what we were anticipating. The total cost—including the uplink and plenty of downlinks—plus the transmission of the games was going to be about 50% more than the new AT&T transmission rates. The uplinks and downlinks were a one-time investment, so we would be saving big-time with the transmissions costs each year. Besides annual cost savings, the sound quality of the satellite transmission was far superior than often-scratchy telephone lines.

Still, to put that cost in perspective, this whole satellite system would have a price tag of one of our star players. It wasn't an either/or situation, of course, but it illustrates that going satellite was a large financial commitment.

There were three folks on our radio in-house staff at that time, so we now had a *team* to create The Outrageous Approval Tool.

During the investigative stage of looking into satellite transmission, we had to learn a new technical language, and none of us were techies. Whatever new language we would learn, we would need to translate it back into simpler language for our presentation.

We worked on The Outrageous Approval Tool for a

few days. The most challenging part wasn't defining the technical aspects. The most difficult part was coming up with the 'Problems' section and anticipating the out-of-left-field questions we would probably get.

We felt that if we stammered and stuttered in answering even one question, particularly a technical question, we could lose the whole deal. We worked at crafting honest logical answers to technical questions from non-technical bosses. We also crafted answers to crazy nobody-would-in-their-right-mind-ask questions.

We made the pitch to the owner of the team and my immediate boss.

After our Summary, there was a short conversation. Then the owner of the team, Larry Weinberg, said (and these were pretty close to his exact words), "Yeah, go ahead with the satellite and that uplink/downlink stuff, but you know that wasn't fair what you did to me to get the approval. There was one question that I thought you would need some time to research. But you answered flawlessly. That's not fair." That wasn't the last time I heard that from a boss.

With satellite transmissions, we were able to add stations in Idaho, Alaska and Hawaii. Our footprint was a lot bigger than just Portland; we were literally and geographically the Northwest's Team.

And then, almost by accident, other syndicated radio shows found out about our satellite network and wanted to rent our transponder. And, boy, did we have a ton of hours we could rent to them. 8,514 hours per year to be exact. Soon, sales from our satellite network paid for our yearly transmission costs and add over $100,000 a year to our bottom line.

Our uplink would shoot our broadcasts up about 22,000 miles to the satellite transponder where it would bounce down those same 22,000 miles to the radio stations on our network, who in turn would broadcast the game to your radio.

CASE STUDY #2: LET'S NOT SELL SOMETHING THAT NOBODY WANTS.

After I left the Portland Trail Blazers, the New Jersey Nets hired me in 1990 as a consultant. The Nets were a hapless, hopeless team that had been dead-last in victories and attendance for seven straight years in the NBA. They hired me to help them sell sponsorships, hoping that I could transfer the success we had in Portland to northern New Jersey. I knew that was not going to be possible and said so to the seven owners.

"I don't want to sound rude," I said, "but who in the world would want to buy a sponsorship with the Nets? Nobody goes to the games, and those who do look like suspects."

"So, what do we do?"

"You have to sell tickets," I said. "A lot of them."

"Who in the world would buy tickets?" one owner blurted out.

That's where we started.

The Nets had less than 500 season ticketholders in an arena that could accommodate 20,000 fans. With a bad team with a predictably bleak future, filling up those empty seats with season ticketholders was not possible.

The written proposal I had prepared looked eerily similar to the format of The Outrageous Approval Tool, although lengthier. It even had the same type of spiral binding. Here's a thumbnail of The Outrageous Approval Tool.

1. **Foreword**. This was a single page. It listed that the Nets had the worst record in the NBA for the past seven seasons. It also listed that they were dead last in attendance in the NBA for those seven seasons. It highlighted that Northern New Jersey, if recognized as a *city*, that it would be the

second-largest city in the United States. Importantly, Northern New Jersey had 20,000 businesses that fit our profile of possible ticket package buyers. As a point of comparison, Portland had less than 5,000 of such companies.

2. **Concept.** I recommended that we shift focus from the traditional team marketing. We would concentrate all efforts *creating sellouts* to specific games and no emphasis on full season tickets. Additionally, we would focus all of our marketing efforts (and I meant *all*) on Northern New Jersey. This meant we would turn our backs on New York City, or in terms of Ulysses, we would put wax in our ears so we couldn't hear the siren song of Manhattan.

I suggested we get sellouts by taking their most popular opponents and putting them into 5-game ticket packages. You know, put Larry Bird and the Celtics, Michael Jordan and the Chicago Bulls, Magic Johnson's LA Lakers and the New York Knicks into one ticket package. By doing this, we would be selling more tickets during the season. Eventually, maybe two-three years later, we would be selling out most of the games and could then target the worst attractions on the schedule. By then, hopefully, the team would be a lot better.

By the way, none of those games had sold out in previous years. Amazingly, the greatest attraction in the NBA, Michael Jordan, sold out every game he played in each season *except* the two he played every season in New Jersey. Michael's games in New Jersey usually had 7,000 empty seats.

There was some stunned silence in the room after I had explained the Concept, but I swung into the next phase, The Rationale.

3. **Rationale**. I made my arguments, using a couple of charts showing how total attendance would increase if we increased attendance to games that featured our most attractive opponents. For example, add 7,000 fans to each Michael Jordan game (2 x 7,000 = 14,000), and 9,000 to each Celtic game (3) games (3 x 9,000 = 27,000) and so forth. Pretty soon, average attendance would increase by 5,000 per game. Not great, but a start.

In this section, I also made the case to focus solely on Northern New Jersey. It was not easy for folks who lived in Manhattan (or the Bronx or Long Island) to come to a Nets game. As expansive as the subway system was in Manhattan, there was no direct line to the Nets arena from Manhattan. If the person drove, they'd have to drive through the Lincoln Tunnel. Really? Do that for a Nets game?

4. **Problems.** I had anticipated that this would be the liveliest part, but surprisingly it wasn't. There were a couple of modest questions, which were easy to field. I felt some serious questions/objections were smoldering below the surface, but they didn't ignite. That was not a good sign.

5. **Summary.** Pretty simple timelines of when to initiate the recommendation.

There was not an animated discussion at the end. The owners wanted a night to think it over. The first thing I did after the meeting was to make sure that my plane reservation to return to Portland the next day was still solid.

We met the next morning. I fully expected them *not* to accept my proposal, and I would collect my consulting fee and head home to Portland, Oregon.

One owner said, "Your proposal made me angry. You went against everything I ever believed in how to market a team. When I got home yesterday, I had to walk around the block to cool down. It didn't work; I was still angry. Then I had to walk around the block three more

times. On the fourth time, I started to think your proposal was a bit of genius. In fact, in the 'Problems' section, you answered every question convincingly. I vote
we do it."

Another owner said, with vigor, "This is way too good
of a deal for our fans."

Yep, I had prepared for a similar objection and was
ready. I pounced, saying, "You've specialized in doing
crappy deals for your fans, and your fans haven't
bought. Let's give them this deal and let them think you
made a *mistake* and that they better buy before you realize your mistake."

That answer brought some laughter.

After 15 minutes of discussion, the seven owners voted:
It was unanimous. That was a rare time all seven owners voted the same on an issue. (There's one other
instance, and I cover that next.)

One of the owners later told me that he had shared
the written proposal with his wife. He had labeled her
'a tough cookie.' He said that she was amazed at how
candid the questions/problems had been in the written
proposal, that they were not laced with 'bs.' She
thought the plan would work, he voted yes, and the
plan did indeed work.

We offered the 5-game packages to fans in Northern
New Jersey. We sold over 25,000 of them! We achieved
five sellouts and were close on a few more. The New
Jersey Nets, who had not had a sellout in seven years,
was now drawing big crowds (for some games). For

the less popular games, nobody knew about the lean crowds. After all, if nobody went to the game, nobody knew that nobody went to the game.

The folks who bought those 5-game plans, however, had a lot of fun at the sold-out arena. They told their friends and families. Two years later, the Nets sold out 29 games and ranked 7th in the NBA for total attendance.

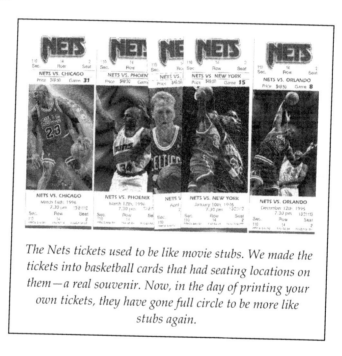

The Nets tickets used to be like movie stubs. We made the tickets into basketball cards that had seating locations on them—a real souvenir. Now, in the day of printing your own tickets, they have gone full circle to be more like stubs again.

CASE STUDY #3: PUTTING A TEAM INTO THE WITNESS PROTECTION PROGRAM.

In this instance, I had to get approval from:

1. My seven bosses, the owners of the New Jersey Nets;

2. David Stern, the commissioner of the NBA;

3. The NBA Executive Committee, which was the 11 most powerful owners;

4. The owners of then twenty-seven NBA teams.

That was the gauntlet. I used The Outrageous Approval Tool every step of the way.

The challenge was to change the nickname of the New Jersey Nets to the New Jersey *Swamp Dragons*. Crazy, eh? It was like taking a team that had a miserable past and putting them in the Witness Protection program.

Well, in a period that took four months and four different approval meetings, we got the approval from each group in what we called The Approval Gauntlet.

With all those approvals, why no New Jersey Swamp Dragons?

Zach Lowe of ESPN.com best tells the story:

Zach Lowe of ESPN.com best tells the story. The easiest way to find the story is to go to Google, type in ESPN Swamp Dragons, and the story will pop up.

If you want to see what the Swamp Dragons uniforms would have looked like, go to YouTube.com on the Internet. In the blank search bar, type in: Swamp Dragons. Press enter. Click on the first video and you've got an interesting video on the graphics of the Swamp Dragons uniforms.

Alas, the New Jersey Swamp Dragons never came to life. Long after I had left the Nets, the team relocated to Brooklyn. They are now the *Brooklyn* Nets. Legend has it that the move to Brooklyn was the curse of the Swamp Dragons.

I submit to you that if the New Jersey Swamp Dragons would have indeed come to life, they probably would still call New Jersey home, and Brooklyn probably would have received an expansion team. Heck, the New Jersey Swamp Dragons could be leading the NBA in licensed product sales, and with their daring name might just be vying for championships.

The moral of this story is that even with an outrageous idea and getting approvals from bosses all over the world, that sometimes things don't work out. But, *the process* of getting The Approval is something that can be a vital tool in getting your next idea approved.

CASE STUDY #4: LET'S INSTALL THE LONGEST TV IN THE WORLD.

I got involved with Minor League Baseball in the early 2000s with a new single-A team, the Dayton Dragons.

Our goal with the Dragons was to sell every ticket to every game in the 7,200-seat stadium. No minor league baseball team had sold out every game in a season in the 100+ year history of Minor League Baseball. (The Dragons achieved that goal, plus sold every ticket to every game for *20 seasons,* surpassing the previous 18-year, 814-game sellout streak I had been a part of with the Portland Trail Blazers. And, Dayton Dragons are *still* selling out.)

Besides selling out every game, we wanted to install the longest TV in the world.

Huh?

In this case, the longest TV in the world was our outfield wall. Our outfield wall was a LED sign. I'm not talking about an occasional LED advertising sign on the wall; I'm talking about *the entire wall*. 9 feet tall, 250 feet wide.

Advertising signs on an outfield wall was the largest source of advertising revenue for minor league baseball teams. Some teams would pack as many advertisers onto these outfield walls as possible. It wasn't unusual to see a team with over 70 different advertisers on its outfield walls. Each advertiser would have about as much space as a grave, four feet by eight feet. In many cases, this small sign was a way for a company to support the local team—sort of a charitable contribution.

Where's the scoreboard?

This is the way many other teams did it.

In Dayton, we felt that we had to differentiate ourselves from all the other minor league teams in regards to potential sponsors. That meant looking at the most valuable piece of advertising real estate—the outfield fence—and doing something dramatically different.

Instead of plastering 70 advertisers on the outfield fence, we decided to have *one* fence sign for *one* advertiser that was *9 feet tall* and stretched *250 feet*.

If you have trouble visualizing 250 feet, think football for a moment. 250 feet represents a little more than 80 yards on the football field.

Besides having the longest outfield fence sign in the history of the world, we decided that the fence should *move*.

We acquired the same type of signage equipment the NBA teams use at their scorer's table. So, at the push of a button, the whole 250-foot sign would light up, changing graphics when directed.

The cost, of course, was crazy. A sign that size would easily cost over $1,000,000. Other teams had an expense of about $10,000 to paint advertising signs on their outfield wall. We were talking more than a cool million. This expense could be considered insane, particularly considering that Dayton, at the time, was a rust-belt city that hadn't yet recovered from a downward economic spiral.

Working with the staff at the Dayton Dragons, we created the proposal using The Outrageous Approval Tool.

Here are the steps we took:

1. **Foreword.** Dayton was a rust-belt city, but

they were enthusiastic about baseball. City leaders championed the construction of a new 7,200 seat downtown ballpark.

2. **Concept.** Instead of selling 70 sponsors to put on the outfield wall, we wanted to sell eight. Each sponsor would be exclusively featured on the 250 wall for one-eighth of the game. (The sign would change between half-innings.)

3. **Rationale.** We explained why eight sponsors were the right number, and that we could sell the smaller sponsors other advertising opportunities. We included financial projections that showed that we needed only to sell one sponsor and that would pay for the outfield wall.

4. **Problems.** We had all types of questions, including what would happen if the outfield wall blew a fuse. (We were prepared for that. We had extra fuses, and folks that knew how to insert them.)

5. **Summary.** Basic timelines needed to sell and then install the longest fence sign in the history of the world.

I made the pitch to the Board of Directors of Mandalay Baseball Properties, the owners. Remember, some things in life are just not fair, and presenting this crazy idea to a Board using The Outrageous Approval Tool was not fair...to the Board.

We got the approval.

You could see the longest TV in the world at a Dayton Dragons games. It was the outfield wall. We liked it so well we did the same thing with our team in Staten Island.

The reception of this concept was fabulous. Potential sponsors looked at us as not just a minor league ball club looking for a charitable donation, but a team of *marketers* who could help *them* dramatically feature their products.

The total revenue from outfield walls for the best minor league teams at that time was about $400,000 a season, less the $10,000 for painting. Our revenue was $1,600,000, less the $130,000 cost to lease the LED equipment.

We liked the drama of the longest TV in the world so much that we adapted it to two other teams we owned. Oh, we also thoroughly enjoyed the revenue too.

CASE STUDY #5: GETTING THE GOVERNMENT TO PAY FOR THE FLOOR OUR SALES STAFF WALKED ON.

The 5-game ticket packages we were selling at the New Jersey Nets were a huge success. We used two ways to market them: 1) Direct response using newspaper ads; 2) a small sales staff. In the first two seasons, our experience showed that we could sell a lot more ticket packages to corporations, but there was one major logistical problem. No, the problem wasn't the need to increase the sales staff. The problem was *where to put* any new salespeople we added.

The Nets' office had been a cramped storage area in the arena. Employees were sharing desks and even phones. There was no room in the arena where we could expand.

Offices were available to rent in a nearby office park.

The Nets owners wouldn't pay for another office because the arena lease included office space. If it was too small, tough luck. To get somebody to pay for it. I went to a source that nobody would have predicted. I went to the government.

In this case, it was the state governing body of the arena, the New Jersey Sports and Exposition Authority, or the NJSEA. They were the Nets' landlord.

I requested a meeting with the NJSEA. They thought I was going to try to renegotiate the team's lease. It was common knowledge that the Nets' lease was the worst in the NBA.

My opening line at the meeting with the NJSEA executives was, "I'm not here to try to renegotiate the lease."

My next line was, "I'm here to make the NJSEA a lot more money."

My next step was something you are now familiar with; I swung into The Outrageous Approval Tool:

1. **Foreword.** This was a 'State of the Nation' about New Jersey Nets ticket sales, which showed a dramatic increase in the previous two seasons. That was good for the NJSEA because they got a small piece of every ticket sold, along with our seasonal game-by-game rent.

2. **Concept**. The main thrust was how the ticket sales improvement could take an even

more significant leap by increasing the sales staff from four to twenty. I showed figures of our successes with selling ticket packages to corporations and how fertile that market was in Northern New Jersey. However, alas, there was no place to put a large sales staff. I wanted them to pay for an office in a nearby office park. The NJSEA would need to pay for the rental space we chose, pay for the rental furniture, and phone system.

3. **Rationale.** I covered what was in it for the NJSEA. While the Nets' lease was a horrible one for the Nets, it was highly profitable for the NJSEA. The NJSEA should have been embarrassed about how they took advantage of the Nets. However, there was an even more gargantuan payday for the NJSEA, which they could never reach without my help. I was there to help them achieve that enormous payday.

That payday would come true if the Nets reached a certain ticket sales plateau that nobody had anticipated when the lease was signed. With a beefed-up sales staff, that number seemed at least something we could dream about.

I showed them the total cost of the new office space. I included the cost of rental furniture, computers, and phones. I also showed them the potential increase in their piece of the gate receipts and concessions if we added salespeople. The NJSEA share could increase by *millions* of dollars.

4. **Problems**. This was the first question: "What happens if we don't buy you a new office?" one of the NJSEA leaders asked.

   "We won't hire that sales staff," I said. "We don't have any place to put them."

   The NJSEA took a few minutes to huddle.

   "Okay, we'll do it," the leader said. "When do you get going on this?"

   "Tomorrow."

We never got to the summary part.

Tomorrow came, and we rented an office that would house twenty ticket sales employees, plus managers. We rented desks and chairs and tables and coffee machines. We leased computers, a network system, and a hi-tech phone system. NJSEA paid for all of it. Gleefully so. Our ticket sales increase went through the roof.

For NJSEA, it was like having three stars lined up on a slot machine, causing lights to flash and bells to ring and a casino employee rushing out and handing them a check worth millions.

Once we hit that plateau, it was rinse and repeat season after season.

Our salesroom wasn't quite like that featured in the movie Wolf of Wall Street, but you get the idea, and the government paid for it.

CASE STUDY #6: I WANT TO BUY YOU DINNER AT EVERY GAME YOU GO TO.

When I was president of Mandalay Baseball Properties, we ended up owning seven minor league baseball teams. One of them was the Staten Island Yankees, a Short-Season Single-A team. The team had had a pitiful record of attendance over their seven years of existence before we purchased them. They had never sold out their 7,000 seat stadium for even one game.

Folks in Staten Island didn't hold back in telling us about our team:

"The area is too dangerous."

"It's *minor* league baseball, and we can go to Yankees or Mets games."

"There's no parking."

Additionally, there was a real shortage in the types of companies that would buy ticket packages. Staten Island was more like a bedroom community to NYC. Our marketing efforts would have to be targeted only to the fans, of which, Staten Island had exhibited very few in the years before.

We felt we had to employ our *secret weapon*, a marketing tactic that we had used with tremendous success with some of our other minor league teams.

This secret weapon was:

> If you buy a 5-game ticket package, you can have all the hot dogs, cheeseburgers, grilled chicken sandwiches, and soda and water you want during the game.

Yep, for a $15 ticket, you could eat all the hotdogs, cheeseburgers, and chicken sandwiches you wanted, washing them down with all the soda and water you could drink. If you wanted to, you could eat us out of house and home. Go ahead, be my guest.

There was one major problem in presenting this ticket package to our fans. We didn't have the right to give away food at our ballpark. Centerplate, the concession-aire in the stadium, held that right.

Centerplate had an airtight contract at the ballpark that seemed to reach a few years beyond eternity. (The previous owner had needed some cash, and the concession-aire gleefully provided it for a better contract with a lengthy extension. It became the worst lease between a team and its concessionaire that I had ever seen.)

Nobody has ever singled out ballpark concessionaires of being great marketers of their food. Concessionaires buy food in bulk, prepare it, sell it, count the money, clean up. That's it. Every one of their executives seems to be a cost accountant—increasing prices and shaving expenses is their lifeblood.

Giving away food would be okay if the team was willing to pay the full price for it. We, of course, wanted to do things differently.

I requested a meeting with Centerplate big-shots.

My opening line at the meeting with the Centerplate executives was, "I'm not here to try to renegotiate the contract."

My next line was, "I'm here to make Centerplate a lot more money." (That may sound like my opening lines to the NJSEA, and it's close, but it works. Try it if you have the chance.)

Here we go:

1. **Foreword.** I outlined the awful attendance record and the dismally low number of hot dogs, sodas, and beers our fans purchased during the previous season.

2. **Concept.** I explained our all-you-can-eat

ticket package. As I talked, I noticed each of the three Centerplate executives fold their arms across their chests. Hard and tight, like they were squeezing something. Not a good sign. The arms tightened a bit more when I explained that we wanted to pay for all this free food at bare product cost, meaning no markups. This, of course, was new math to a concessionaire.

3. **Rationale.** Here's how the new math would work. Back in 2007 a hot dog could be purchased at a concession stand for $6. Of that price, Centerplate kept $4.20; the team got $1.80. For our all-you-can-eat ticket package, we wanted to pay just the real cost of the hot dog, or 64 cents each. For a $3 bottle of water, we wanted to just pay the 34 cent real cost.

I explained what was in it for them.

We would probably sell more than 10,000 of these all-you-can-eat ticket plans. I showed them numbers where we had done that with two of our other teams.

I said, "With each fan who comes in, each one brings a *mouth*. And a *stomach*. Our history shows they will want something more than hotdogs and a soda. They'll want beer and peanuts and cotton candy and ice cream and pizza. Even though we gave away all this free food at our other teams, the average fan still spent $10 more for food and beverage."

I asked Centerplate how much people were spending on food at a Staten Island game.

One guy murmured, "Less than three dollars." It's a strange phenomenon, but true—people eat less at games with a sparse attendance than when there is a big crowd.

Even with my new math, Centerplate wasn't sure it was a good idea for them. Concessionaires are a tough bunch. However, I did have an ace in the hole.

"As you know," I said, "a different concessionaire with a separate kitchen on the second level serves the 22 suites in the ballpark. I think that's crazy to have two concessionaires in the same building."

They nodded their heads in agreement.

"But, we are going to do the all-you-can-eat ticket package, and if need be, I'll have the fans climb the stairs to the suite level to get their free food. You'll still benefit greatly by having a big increase of fans, and we'll be able to do our all-you-can-eat ticket package, but as you know, that wouldn't be the right thing to do. There should be only one concessionaire in the stadium."

Centerplate asked if they could get the concession rights to the suite level if they participated in our all-you-can-eat ticket plan. I'm sure they knew that the concessionaire on the suite level was a buddy of the previous owner and didn't have an agreement.

I said, "I think it's right to have just one concessionaire, but as we have discussed, you took the previous owner to the cleaners. You should be ashamed of taking advantage of that guy. If we're bringing in tens of thousands of new fans, and we grant you the right to suite level, it seems the right thing to do would be to adjust our deal."

They agreed. We cut a new deal where, with significant increases in attendance, our commission on food sales would increase from 30% to 50%. That wasn't as good of a deal as we had with other teams, but they really didn't have to give us any increase.

4. **Problems**. It seemed at this point that

Centerplate was willing to go with our all-you-can-eat ticket package because almost all of the questions were about logistics. You know, where would we want to free food buffet line, where would we positioned the beer kiosks, etc.

5. **Summary**. This was mostly timelines, and I noticed that Centerplate execs had unfolded their arms and were nodding their heads.

That first year, we sold over 15,000 of those all-you-eat-ticket plans. The average cost to the team for all that free food and drink and labor was about $3.50 per person. Subtract the food/beverage cost from the $15 ticket, and it gave us a net of $11.50 per ticket sold. That was 50 cents more than the list price of the ticket from the year before.

Yes, we had raised the ticket price from $11 to $15. There were no complaints about raising the ticket prices because if nobody was going to the games, nobody knew what nobody wasn't paying to not go to the games.

Centerplate did terrific also. We sold out 20 of 36 home games providing Centerplate thousands upon thousands of mouths to feed.

All the hotdogs, cheeseburgers, and chicken sandwiches you can eat, plus all the water and soft drinks for free wasn't very appealing to a concessionaire. Until they found out what a great deal it was for them.

This is a full-page ad in The New York Daily News. For every dollar it cost us to run it, we got eight dollars back in ticket sales.

9

A short chapter on shortcuts

I would have loved taking a shortcut to get the approval from my boss.

But, I never found any shortcuts.

It's not like I haven't thought of inventing some shortcuts. Heck, the work in preparing The Outrageous Approval Tool is often daunting. It has caused me some sleepless nights during the days of preparation. It gave me headaches that weren't cured by Excedrin, particularly when I asked myself, "What questions have we overlooked in the 'Problems' section?"

Overlook just one lousy question—even an off-the-wall stupid question that could only be asked by a lunatic—and it could derail approval.

So, alas, I never was able to come up with a shortcut for The Outrageous Approval Tool. (If, however, you come up with a real doable shortcut, please let me know.)

10

Rinse and repeat

I illustrated six Case Studies where I had used The Outrageous Approval Tool to get my bosses to approve what I wanted to do. I chose those six because of the diversity—and the seeming craziness—of each idea.

Each time I got the approval, and each time it was a rousing success, with the lone exception being the silliness of the aborted New Jersey Swamp Dragons. (I still count the Swamp Dragons a success because we did indeed get the approval from a gauntlet of bosses. And, the Swamp Dragons will forever live in marketing lore.)

So, how many times did I go back to the well and drag out The Outrageous Approval Tool?

You might be surprised. Not that often. Over 30+ years, I used The Outrageous Approval Tool just one dozen times. You may wonder why only 12? Here's the only reason why:

THE ONLY REASON

The Only Reason: Use it for only the big stuff, the

stuff that can materially change what you do for a living, or even change your life.

Most decisions, in business and life, can be made with relative ease. You choose one thing, or you select the other. Italian restaurant tonight or Chinese? The net result, regardless of the one you chose, doesn't make that much of a difference.

However, let's take a quick look at my first example, bringing radio in-house. That decision changed *my career*. That one decision catapulted my career, not only with the team I was with but with other teams and even leagues in other sports and other countries.

If I hadn't taken the time to prepare The Outrageous Approval Tool, the Trail Blazers probably wouldn't have brought radio in-house. I would have had a career in selling small ads on the backs of ticket envelopes.

That would not have been enough for me, even though working for a pro sports team was a blast. I probably would have been frustrated and soon would have been looking for another job.

Each time I used The Outrageous Approval Tool, my career was helped. When I sit back and take an objective look, I conclude I had a much better career by getting my boss to approve things I wanted to do than if I just went with the status quo.

11

Does it always work?

Yes, The Outrageous Approval Tool always works. But, there is an important *if*.

That important 'if' is *if* you provide the strenuous effort.

Are you willing to prepare as if you were preparing to save your life in front of your Supreme Court?

I used The Outrageous Approval Tool only 12 times total in my career. 12 times I went in front of my Supreme Court, and, 12 times, I got the approval. Each of those approvals created vital milestones for me.

Some of the 'Justices' on my Supreme Court were not sympathetic at all to me or my ideas, and they weren't anxious to give me the approval. In a few cases, it was probably *painful* for them to provide me with the approval.

The most surprising part of the whole process was how *easy* it was to get the approval, and how *quickly* the approval came after the presentation. How cool is that?

Sure, the preparation was not easy. The 'Problems' section was particularly challenging to prepare. Each problem had to have a straight declaration of what the problem was, and a straightforward explanation of how we would handle that problem if it arose. The answer could not even hint of hype, and I would have to deliver the effectively answer without hesitation.

Some might consider that I used it only when I had a really crazy idea and that moderately-insane ideas didn't need such work. The degree of preparation wasn't my yardstick. I used The Tool only when the idea was big enough to warrant the fear of not being able to do something that I wanted to do. For example, *not* bringing radio in-house would have been awful for me.

Or, *not* selling 5-game ticket packages in New Jersey, and concentrating only on selling full season tickets would have created sure failure, which I, of course, didn't want to be a part of. Instead of experiencing failure in New Jersey, my career was enhanced by the Nets' wildly unorthodox rise of ticket sales in the NBA.

You'll find that if you thoroughly prepare—and I mean a preparation like you're going to the Supreme Court to save your life—approvals will come pretty quickly without too much pushback.

12

When to sit on it

The Outrageous Approval Tool *never* failed when I used it to present an idea to my boss.

However, during the preparation of The Outrageous Approval Tool, we would sometimes find severe flaws in the idea. We never saw those flaws during the incubation of the idea. We worked hard to try and fix those flaws, trying one alternative solution after another. But, on two occasions, there was no elixir.

In both instances, the fatal flaw was discovered well into the preparation of The Outrageous Approval Tool. When an idea had a fatal flaw, and we couldn't save it, we would reluctantly bury it. Out of respect for the doomed idea, we would host a wake, hoisting a few beers in honor of the idea that we thought had break-through genes.

While there was no solace in burying an idea, we were pleased that we had even come up with the idea and pursued the development of it.

We were also pleased that we uncovered the fatal flaw before we had set up a meeting with the boss. If we hadn't discovered that fatal flaw, you can bet your house that the boss would have done so during the pitch.

We took particular comfort in the thought of the damage we avoided if the boss missed spotting the fatal flaw, and the idea came to life and flopped miserably.

13
Making it work for you

What if you do *not* have an idea that you consider important enough that you need your boss' approval?

You may have a wonderful boss who is providing a fantastic work environment filled with new ideas and fun challenges. Relish that time. Enjoy!

But, let's say an idea creeps into your consciousness—a really cool idea—and you want to see it come to life.

I ask you, "How important is that idea to you?"

You say, "Very important."

You add, "I'm starting to feel that this idea could be essential to my career. It's that important."

I ask, "What if your boss rejects the idea?"

You answer, "My boss wouldn't do that. My boss is wonderful and creative and a true visionary."

I wouldn't want to dampen your spirit—and with all due respect to your boss—but I wouldn't trust my idea with *any* boss, saintly boss or otherwise, without using The Outrageous Approval Tool.

The boss might just be having a bad day the day you ask for approval in a casual way. You get a rejection, and once rejected, it's very difficult to resuscitate it.

I ask, "Is the idea important enough to prepare as if you're presenting it to the Supreme Court to save your life?"

You're really choosing between 1) a surefire approval with The Outrageous Approval Tool or 2) a chance—maybe slim—that it won't be approved with a casual approach.

You nod your head and say, "I don't want to risk the approval. I going to use The Outrageous Approval Tool."

"Are there people in your organization who share with you this idea and would love for it to be approved?" I ask you. There is no right or wrong answer to this question. I've gone solo with an idea (radio in-house), and I've gone with a team of three (get our own satellite), and I've gone with five or more (longest TV screen in the world and the Witness Protection team).

If you're doing it solo, you have to do all the thinking, all the writing, all the prep work. That's okay; it's your idea; it's your career.

If you're working with a small group, you've got collaborators. That's okay, too; it's now *our* idea; it's *our* careers. You only want people in the group with close to the same passion and dedication that you put into it.

Whenever I worked with a small group, I led the strategy meetings. We would discuss each of the segments that would go into The Outrageous Approval Tool. We would police each other to make sure we weren't making inflated claims that would be difficult to believe. A group is particularly useful when working on the 'Problems' section.

Whether you're solo or with a small group, here is a step-by-step plan in preparing The Outrageous Approval Tool:

STEP #1
___

When you start to prepare The Outrageous Approval Tool, begin with the *second* part—*The Concept* first. Just write down what your idea is. Plain and simple, without hype, without exclamation points. This section should be about one page, no more than two. The *Concept* is a general overview of your idea. Be succinct.

How solid do you feel your idea is? If you're unsure, then sleep on it for a couple of days. Revisit what you have written. Do you find yourself nodding your head in approval? If so, move to the next step. (If not, take a little more time to shape your idea. If it never feels right, or never reads right, you might want to shelve the idea for a while and revisit it a month or so later. I've got a file folder of shelved ideas. Only go with the big idea that you *really* want to get approved.)

STEP #2
___

Once you are satisfied with the Concept section, you

start on The *Foreword,* which is, of course, the first part of The Outrageous Approval Tool. You may find that this section is easier to write than the Concept. It's like you're writing a snatch of history. You're stating as factual as possible what condition the market and your organization is in. You're not trying to shade history here; if you do attempt shading it, your Supreme Court could call you out on it. A debate, or even worse an argument, could emerge. Not good. That could put a dent in your credibility even before you get to pitch your idea. Play it straight.

STEP #3

Why in the world should your organization adopt your idea? This is the *Rationale* section. You have to have good-to-excellent reasons here. If the reasons for adopting your idea are lukewarm, then you probably will get a lukewarm answer, which is not an approval. It's a "Thanks, we'll think about it" response, and the idea will end up stored in some dusty file cabinet.

If it's about *increasing revenue,* then you have to state here your reasonable expectation of how much. The amount should be relatively conservative—a number that you should be able to reach if your idea is approved. With my 'radio in-house' idea with the Portland Trail Blazers, I put in an impressive increase (raising profit from radio from $25,000 to $100,000) that I thought I could easily reach). As it turned out, my number was way conservative, with the actual results coming in at almost $900,000.

After you explain how much you feel your idea could increase revenue, you could insert a pro forma statement to illustrate how profitable this new revenue would be.

If it's about *saving money*, then state how much would be saved by implementing the idea. Again, a pro forma statement would help illustrate your point.

STEP #4

I often think this is the most vital part of The Outrageous Approval Tool. *Problems*. The Problems section is a catch-all section that covers possible current problems in initiating the idea, as well as future problems, unforeseen problems, never-could-happen-in-a-million-years problems. 'Problems' also mean objections or just cranky questions. If you get headaches preparing this segment, don't worry. It's part of the process.

This step is so important—even more so than the others— because problems can derail you in a flash. If you don't have the quick and decisive answer to a question and you stammer or just wing it, your idea could go *poof before your very eyes*.

Some of the problems or potential problems are relatively easy to identify. So, start with those. Write them down—as a non-biased observer would—and write down the answers in a straightforward way that even a jerk couldn't challenge.

That's the easy part. Now let's do something more challenging.

Imagine the ultimate cross-examiner, perhaps somebody like Vincent Bugliosi, the Los Angeles District Attorney, who got Charles Manson convicted. Or imagine somebody you know who is a great questioner. The best I've ever come across was Larry Weinberg, the owner of the Portland Trail Blazers during most of my years there. Larry rarely asked the *obvious* questions. No, his were several layers beyond that. So, when I was working on preparing The Outrageous Approval Tool, I always thought, "What questions would Larry ask?" I'd write out answers to those questions, which would be direct and not too wordy.

I met one other person who was the master of asking questions. I had first met this guy when I was president of the New Jersey Nets. He knew some of the owners of the Nets, and he would occasionally come to a game, and we'd have casual conversations in the owner's suite during the games. One day, he phoned me direct (no assistant or secretary placing his call) and said, "I'm thinking about buying a Major League Baseball team. I was wondering if you could come over and talk to me about what I might be getting into."

I said, "Sure." A few days later, I drove over to Manhattan and went to the 26th floor of the Trump Tower and was ushered into the office of Donald Trump.

There was no chit-chat to start the meeting.

Donald Trump told me about his interest in buying an unnamed baseball team. He asked me about some pitfalls in owning a Major League Baseball team.

"Do you want me to tell you the truth, or do you want me to feed your ego?" I said, half-jokingly.

His answer was straightforward. "The truth, no sugar-coating."

We discussed the possible project for two hours. (I was told later by a guy who knew such things that Donald Trump rarely had meetings that lasted for more than 15 minutes.)

My lasting thought of the meeting was that I had never met anybody before (or since) who *listened* so *intensely*, almost unnervingly so. His questions became more sophisticated by leaps and bounds as we discussed the project. If I were to work on The Outrageous Approval Tool today for an idea I wanted my boss to approve, I would probably enlist the visage of Donald Trump to ask the tough questions.

If appropriate, I also would imagine an Attila the Hun type of boss. A screamer, a bang-the-desk type. You never know which idea will bring out the Attila in a boss. I think of Leonard Lavin of Alberto-Culver—the guy who scared me witless into creating the first version of The Outrageous Approval Tool. In the safety of your own office, ask yourself the questions your version of Attila the Hun would ask.

So, for this essential step, you might consider enlisting the help from the visage of folks you do know (your boss, your boss's boss and the most skeptical person on your team. You're allowed to bring in ringers into this process, so feel free to bring in the visage of folks you don't know like Leonard Lavin, Vincent Bugliosi, Larry Weinberg, Donald Trump and Attila the Hun. What questions would these people ask about your idea?

STEP #5

You're almost at the finish line. You've made your arguments and have faced the cross-examination by your Supreme Court. There's no more pitching to be done. Step #5 is a *Call for Approval*.

The Call for Approval should have a *specific timetable for approval and implementation*. It shouldn't be more than one or two paragraphs.

A real danger here is *not* including a specific timetable. Without a specific timeframe, the decision easily could be postponed by 'let's think about it' or 'check out this component (whatever that may be), and then we'll see.' That's letting your boss off the hook.

I've faced the 'think about it' gambit only once. That time was when I was a consultant and met with the seven owners of the New Jersey Nets where I recommended not to sell something that nobody wanted (full season tickets), but to sell something that fans would wildly want to buy (five-game plans to our most important games).

They wanted a day 'to think about it among themselves.' If I had been a betting man, I would have bet my house that they would turn down the idea of selling something that fans wildly wanted to buy. It was just so different, and like most bosses, it was easier to say no to an idea than to answer yes.

The next day they told me they loved the idea and asked when I could start to get it implemented. Perhaps this was a case of desperate men doing desperate things.

Because of the Nets owners delaying for a night, I vowed to always plan for The Answer, "We want to think about it."

Just as I prepared for regular questions and some off-the-wall questions, I now would prepare an answer if the boss said, "I need a day to think about it."

This would be my prepared answer, "In the day you want to think about it, and after you ran through all the plusses and the minuses, which way do you think you would be *inclined* to go?"

I'm not asking the boss which way the boss would go—yes or no—but what was the *inclination*. That's like a *lean*, not a hard-fast decision.

If the boss answered, "I'd have to do a little more thinking about it, but I'm inclined to go ahead with it."

I would say, "Terrific, let's get started on it today. You're the boss; you can always pull me off of it. Let's get going today."

If the boss answered, "I don't think I would go ahead with it."

I would ask, "What seemed to be the biggest reason for not going ahead?"

If the boss states a specific problem, that is probably the real obstacle. It's now in the open. Not to worry. You've already prepared for that off-the-wall question or problem, right? If not, see Step #4 and read again. Since you've already prepared to answer your boss's crazy question or real problem, don't hesitate, answer it right away. You'll probably be very persuasive since you've already rehearsed answering that problem.

Maybe the boss didn't fully understand a particular aspect of your presentation, and the question clearly indicates that. Terrific! Now you have the chance to fix that.

If the boss doesn't give you a reason, you have to ask why the hesitation. You *need* an answer. The answer can't be something nebulous.

(If the boss didn't give you any answer for something so essential to you—or an answer that was so foolish that it was embarrassing—I would probably start to think that maybe I should look for other opportunities elsewhere. Hey, just saying, but it's a career we're talking about.)

You might get what *seems* to be a perfectly good reason why your boss cannot approve your idea at that time. Ha! You've already prepared for that reason in Step #4, right? Use that perfectly prepared answer to why your organization should go ahead as planned on the timetable.

If it seems too pushy, yeah, it probably is. But, this is the time to be uncomfortable. If the boss wants to delay, you have to know the reason. If the boss divulges the reason, you probably have the convincing rebuttal that you prepared days before. So, *be uncomfortable. Find the reason for any delay.* You have the rebuttal that will work.

EXPECT AND GET IMMEDIATE APPROVALS

Of the 12 times I've used The Outrageous Approval Tool, I got an immediate approval 11 times. (The lone one-day delay for approval was the New Jersey Nets. The idea of changing the Nets name to Swamp Dragons took *months*, but there were four layers of decisions with one meeting leading to another group meeting weeks later, which, finally led to a quick approval at each meeting.)

A scorekeeper, however, might say that the effort to change the New Jersey Nets name to New Jersey Swamp Dragons was a failure. Okay, the revised score of getting approvals from bosses would be 11 out of 12 tried, or an approval rate of 92%.

EXPECT AND GET FAST APPROVALS

You've got three good reasons to expect fast approvals:

1. **It ain't pie in the sky.** Even if your idea was highly unusual—I'm talking about it being way out of left-field—you proved during your pitch that your idea was rational, realistic, and well-grounded. (Renting a satellite for our radio transmissions seemed really bizarre to me, but as we worked on

The Outrageous Approval Tool, it started to sound and feel sensible, logical, doable, and approvable.) An idea that starts a bit crazy—and the breakthrough ones often do—will take on a normalcy and legitimacy as you work on The Outrageous Approval Tool.

2. **You got a believable rationale down pat, and you know how to handle the problems that may occur.** You demonstrated this in your pitch. Bosses love employees who are that well-prepared.

3. **You made it easier for the boss to say yes than to say no.** In most cases, it's a heckuva lot easier for a boss to say no. After all, with a 'no' answer, nobody sticks their neck out with a new idea, including your boss.

Bosses don't want to look bad with *their* boss, and a flimsy idea that failed could shift the blame back on the boss. Using The Outrageous Approval Tool allows the boss to feel comfortable with your idea, minimizing any danger, making it logical to proceed full-steam ahead.

14

If you think it's safe, watch out!

Imagine that your boss gives you The Approval.

Strange, but when I got The Approval, I don't recall if I had a sense of wild jubilation. Instead, my feelings were that the first step (the approval) had been taken; now it was time to take the second step, then the third step and so forth. Because I prepared to get the approval, my next steps were obvious to me.

What was not obvious was the danger ahead. While your boss did indeed give you the approval, there will be a time during the process where your boss will get cold feet. How cold? It could be just a chill where the boss would want to modify some small components of the idea. With some smooth assurances, you should be able to warm up the boss's feet, not making any changes that would hurt the project.

Or, it could be a deep freeze where the boss would like to kill the idea altogether. This has happened to me—in one form or another—more than a few times after I got the boss to approve a big project.

The best example of the Deep Freeze would be the last

second torpedoing of the nickname change of the New Jersey Nets to the Swamp Dragons. In case you didn't read the ESPN story about the Swamp Dragons, here's another chance for you. Go to Google and type in: ESPN Swamp Dragons. You'll find the story interesting, funny and amazing.

Yep, after all those tough approvals—from Commissioner David Stern to the seven Nets owners to the powerful NBA Executive Committee—it came down to a fax vote from all of the 27 NBA teams. It had been customary that whatever the Executive Committee approved, the rest of the teams would also. All it took was a majority—fourteen votes. It was as much of a done-deal as anything could be. Heck, the NBA had spent hundreds of thousands of dollars registering the name and logo in over 100 countries.

Then one fine spring day, I got a phone call from David Stern.

"What the hell is going on over there?" David shouted.

"What do you mean?" I said.

"We took the vote today for the Swamp Dragons," David said. "It came in at 26-to-1 in favor of changing the nickname."

"Terrific," I said. This wasn't surprising because I had been assured that this fax vote was going to be a slam dunk, in NBA parlance.

"The one dissenting vote, however, was *you guys*! The New Jersey Nets!" David screamed.

He explained how the seven Nets owners would rotate the fax vote on various issues. I didn't know that. The one owner who got the vote that day got cold feet and voted no.

"It doesn't make any difference," I said. "The vote was *26-to-1 in favor*. Forget the Nets vote. 26 other teams voted 'yes.'"

"It's not that easy," David said. "We can't proceed to change the nickname of your team when you guys voted *not* to change it."

Here's what gnaws at me to this day. It's not the decision by that lone owner with frigid feet. What gnaws at me is that I didn't know that the vote was happening on that particular day, nor that I knew the Nets owners rotated the vote, nor that I knew which owner was voting that day. If I had known, I would have been with that owner to hold his hand, assuring him that the name change was going to be terrific for him and his partners. I'm positive that if I had been with him, he would have voted yes.

I had been living in a fantasy where everybody said it was a done-deal. Not so. As Yogi berra might have said, "A deal isn't a deal until it's a signed done-deal."

I should have been more alert to the details of this final vote because I know with any idea that has been approved, there's always a boss that gets some degree of cold feet. In our preparation, particularly the Problems section, we drew up 'Cold Feet Scenarios.' We never drew up the scenario where one of our owners would vote no. I thought the game was won when there were still seconds left on the clock. Shame on me. My unforced turnover.

Yogi Berra said, "It ain't over till it's over."

"Don't count your chickens before they hatch," said a 16th century visionary.

"It ain't over until the fat lady sings," said Don Meredith, a color commentator on Monday Night Football in the 1970s.

"The one detail you overlook could be the one that kills the great idea," said Jon Spoelstra.

Alas, cold feet was the deathknell for the New Jersey Swamp Dragons.

15

You're the boss giving the approval

A weird thing happened to me on my way of becoming a boss.

Once I became a boss with a department full of people reporting to me, I became more skeptical about other people's ideas. God help me, but when I became a boss, I started to *think* like a boss.

Let me explain.

I first realized I was thinking like a boss when an employee would stop me in the hallway and say, "I've got this idea…" You can't believe how delighted I was to hear those words. I love ideas!

The employee would then proceed to tell me about it. Before they completely fleshed out the idea, I would see serious problems with the idea. I'm talking about *fatal* issues.

I would, alas, even develop the killshot by saying, "Have you thought of…" and I would itemize the severe problem.

"Uh…no," the response would often be. Idea DBA: Dead Before Arrival.

It's not that I wanted to kill ideas. Remember, I love ideas! I was often the champion of ideas! How could I explain to myself that I was so rugged on somebody else's ad hoc ideas presented in a hallway?

I think my seeming recent aversion to ideas had come from The Outrageous Approval Tool. You see, I had blissfully and successfully used The Outrageous Approval Tool a few times. Those successes were instrumental in my becoming a boss with employees reporting to me. With the process of using The Outrageous Approval Tool, I think an internal antenna in my brain unlocked to ferret out problems of newly born ideas. Was I now facing a curse or an opportunity?

I chose opportunity.

The opportunity was to unleash the creative thinking of those who worked for me. I have always encouraged ideas, but now I was going to get on a soapbox and invite them to *create ideas*. But, I was also going to have each employee attend a special class. I would teach that class. The title of the course was: How to Get Anything Approved by Your Boss (me).

We didn't have a textbook. If we did, it would be exactly what you're reading now. I would have made it mandatory reading.

16

You don't need anybody's approval. Hah!

I was an entrepreneur before I worked for other companies. One such entrepreneurial effort started when I was in college.

Back in the mid-1960s, colleges often recommended their students buy a desk mat/blotter, which would protect the desktop from any spills, mainly ink from leaky pens. Yep, we used ink pens back then.

These desk mat/blotters would cost about a dollar or two at the campus bookstore. I decided to give away desk mats for free. Printed on the desk mats would be a calendar and football and basketball schedules. And, around the perimeter would be a bunch of small ads from local stores around the campus. I would sell the ads, lay them out in pencil, and work with a printer to print them up.

One college I went to was Marshall University in Huntington, West Virginia. My first sales call was to the local bank. I got to see the president. I gave him my sales pitch why his bank's ad should be on the desk of every student at Marshall.

When I was about to give the price of such an advertisement, the president said, in a marvelous southern drawl, "Sonny, I can be a nice guy, or I can be a sum' bitch."

I said, after a quick swallow, "Well, I've got two prices—one for nice guys and one for…"

I never got to finish the sentence because the president was laughing so hard.

He then said, "How much does it cost if I buy *all* the ads?"

I told him.

He extended his hand and said, "Deal."

For the moment, I was rich!

If only being an entrepreneur could always be that easy. After all, *I* decided which colleges to go to set up my desk mat program. *I* decided the price of the ads, and how many desk mats to print. Heck, *I* decided *everything*.

The desk mat venture was the last time I didn't need to get an approval from somebody somewhere in my business process.

Many, many years later, I became an entrepreneur again. Did I have the same freedom in making decisions as I did with my desk mat program? Of course not. This time I had a business partner, Steve DeLay. I first hired

Steve as a ticket salesperson back with the New Jersey Nets, and then hired him as Chief Marketing Officer of our Mandalay baseball teams. After almost two decades of working with each other, we formed SRO Partners, LLC.

In this partnership, both Steve and I were used to employing The Outrageous Approval Tool, particularly the 'Problems' section. We had trained ourselves over the years to be able to sniff out the problems. So, when we were thinking of initiating something new, we went through the familiar steps in getting approval from ourselves.

Other entrepreneurs have told me that while they might have the final say in a big decision, they go through similar getting-the-approval steps as Steve and I would. However, the one thing lacking in that preparation, many would tell me, was the 'Problems' section. They just wouldn't dig deep enough.

I recommend to those entrepreneurs to take an extra day and write down all the crazy scenarios that could happen in the 'Problems' section. Then write the answers. You want to get the approval from the toughest boss in the room. You.

As business partners, Steve Delay and I employed The Outrageous Approval Tool to help us decide on creating the Macon Bacon baseball team.

17

What does it look like?

The Outrageous Approval Tool is not a big production deal.

I produced them using Microsoft Word and Microsoft Excel. They were mostly black & white. The exception was the New Jersey Swamp Dragons name change, complete with colorful depictions of the logo and uniforms.

The following is what The Outrageous Approval Tool looked like. This proposal was for all-you-can-eat ticket for the Frisco Roughriders, a Double-A minor league baseball team. It was presented to the Board of Directors of Mandalay Baseball for approval.

Straightforward, no fluff.

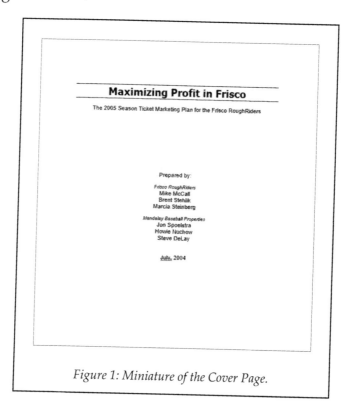

Figure 1: Miniature of the Cover Page.

Frisco Roughriders 2005 Ticket Marketing Plan   JAN. 2004

Contents

1. **Foreword**
   In 2003, Frisco was the most successful minor league team ever. Where do we stand now? Where will we stand next season?

2. **Concept: Reversing Premium Seats Sales Slippage**
   There was major slippage in premium seat renewals and sales. These premium areas demand our top priority.

3. **Rationale: Value Added Premium Seats**
   There are two critical components in reversing the slide of premium ticket sales. One is SportService, the other is sales manpower.

4. **Serious Questions**
   Here are some answers to some tough questions.

5. **Summary** .... Page 38
   The role model we have to look at is us.

Marketing Enabled Properties   Page 1

Figure 2: Miniature of Table of Contents Page.

The situation in Frisco here was more complicated than normal, so the Foreword section took more than the usual 1-2 pages. Here's the first page of the Foreword:

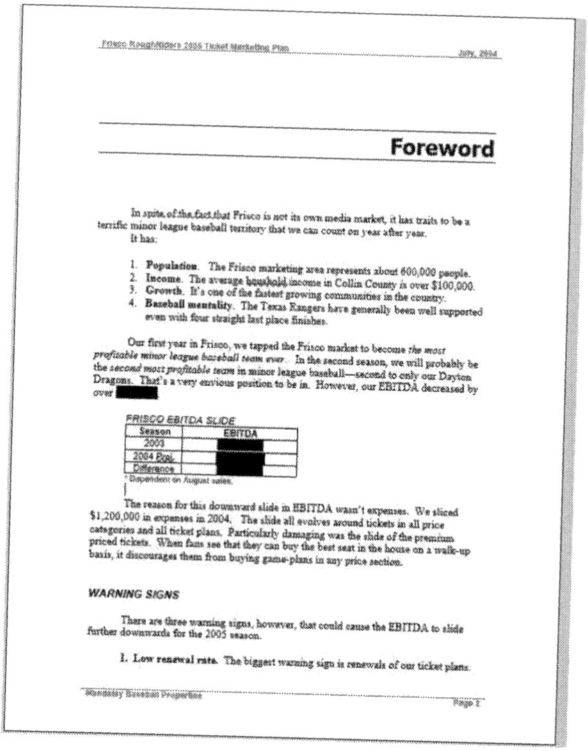

Figure 3: Miniature of the Foreword Section.

Explaining the concept which included charts took three pages.

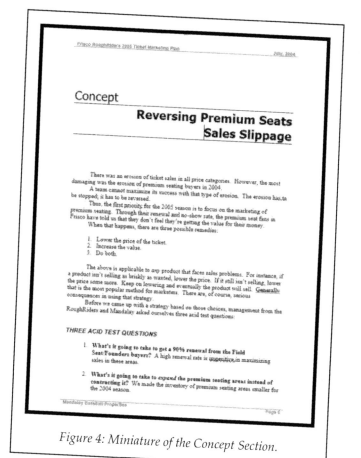

Figure 4: Miniature of the Concept Section.

Here it comes—we explain why we should do this. Three pages.

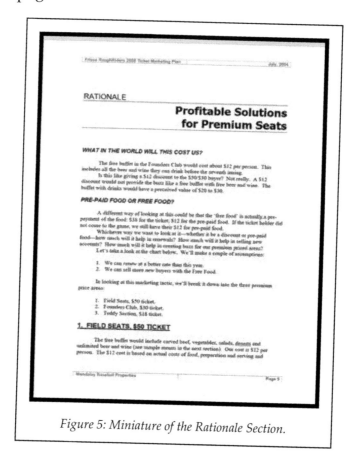

Figure 5: Miniature of the Rationale Section.

This might be the most important section:

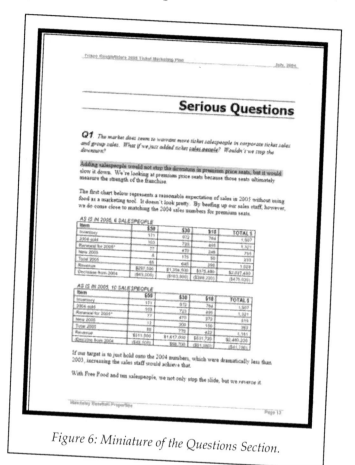

Figure 6: Miniature of the Questions Section.

After five pages of answered questions, the Summary took one and a half pages.

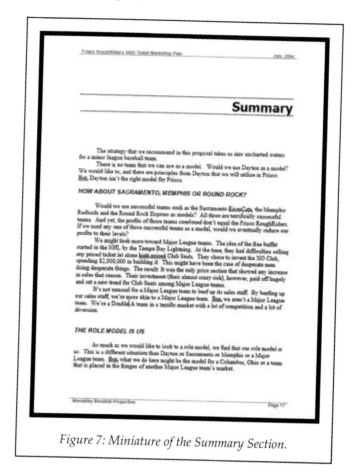

Figure 7: Miniature of the Summary Section.

The Outrageous Approval Tool *looked* professional. More important than looks, however, is the content.

Imagine a hidden decision-maker was handed The Outrageous Approval Tool and asked, "Tell me what you think." What would that hidden decision-maker think? What if the grammar in the document was fifth-grade material? What if there were misspellings galore? And what if there WAS A LOT OF HYPE FOR GOD'S SAKE!!!!!!?

What would the hidden decision-maker think if The Outrageous Approval Tool was a no BS document with the writing being clear and precise?

What if it also seemed to answer every question that could come up?

What if there wasn't much hype or exclamation points or ALL CAPS?

What if even though the idea was highly unusual, it did seem to be a sound idea?

If you're going to spend the time preparing The Outrageous Approval Tool, you don't need the looks and style to derail you. Be careful of the small details.

18

When to take the leap

When is it too early to start preparing The Outrageous Approval Tool?" one person asked me after I had given a speech about this.

"When is it too late?" another person asked.

There were two easy answers.

The answer to 'too early' is: "Get the idea first. Then proceed immediately to the preparation of The Outrageous Approval Tool."

As you get fully into the preparation, you'll get a real feeling on the *speed* you should take. There have been times when I felt I had to finish The Outrageous Approval Tool and make the presentation in a week. It was hot! Other times, I felt the timing could be more relaxed, and I would need to make the pitch in a couple of months. Let your instincts be your guide on how fast you proceed.

The answer to 'too late' is more difficult. I do think there is an expiration date on ideas. I'll give you an obvious example, let's say you came up with the idea of adding bar codes to every retail product. Sorry, that's too late.

However, let's say there's been a specific idea rolling around in your brain for a few years and nobody had created a similar idea. If that's the case with you, you should proceed to the preparation of The Outrageous Approval Tool right away. Remember, most ideas have an expiration date.

The 'too late' questioner then said, "But, I'm in a toxic situation at work. My boss would kill me during the presentation."

If it's a great idea, but looks first-blush crazy and you've got a toxic boss, I would still prepare that idea in The Outrageous Approval Tool. Heck, I've had toxic bosses approve some of my ideas. One way to make them a bit less toxic is to provide them with a truly fleshed out idea that ultimately makes them look good, which your idea could.

If your boss is way too toxic, I would still prepare The Outrageous Approval Tool.

I would use it in my interviews for my next job.

19

How much time invested?

The preparation time for a case to the United States Supreme Court can be extreme, often *years*.

Thank goodness that appealing to our own Supreme Courts doesn't have similar timelines. For me, the longest prep time from start to approval was about four months (New Jersey Swamp Dragons gambit), but they represented *four layers* of approvals from 46 different people. This wasn't continual work for four months, of course, but we had to attend to it off-and-on during that time frame.

A better example of the timeline is the first Case Study—the crazy one about using a satellite transponder to distribute our games to our network of radio stations. There were four of us at the Portland Trail Blazers that were involved in that effort, and none of us knew *anything* about satellite transmissions.

So, we first had to do a lot of homework to find out if there was a financial saving in the idea. Our flagship radio station gave us some names to call, and those names led us to more names. Within a week, we had a pretty good idea of how much money we could save if we went satellite.

Getting firm bids on costs of the satellite dishes, including installations and the costs of the yearly rental of a satellite transponder, took another ten days or so. Thus far, the total human-hours for four people spent on this wild project was probably in the range of 12-15 hours over a period of almost three weeks.

It was only then that we saw the complete—and very bright—picture of what this procedure would mean for the Blazers. "Wow!" We said in unison.

Then it was on to prep time.

It only took me an hour or so to write Part 1 (the Foreword), Part 2 (the Concept) and Part 3 (the Rationale). I handed out a copy to the other three 'co-conspirators' for them to proof and edit, and the next day I incorporated their suggestions.

We then had a meeting that started at 3 pm and didn't end until after 8 pm. That was the meeting when we created Part 4 (Problems), or as we got to know this section as 'Questions, Objections & Other Phenomena.' As you know, I considered this section to be the most important. If we weren't prepared to answer every question—even the absurd—with conviction and confidence, then we could get beat.

I printed out what we had and told everybody to sleep on it.

We spent two hours the next day in firming up Part 4.

Part 5 (Summary) was easy, and I wrote that in 30 minutes.

All four of us weren't going to be making the presentation. It was going to me and my 'technical advisor,' Berl Hodges, who had all the satellite data.

I prepped a few hours over the weekend on what would be my pitch. On Monday, Berl and I went through a dry-run with the other two.

A week later, we made the pitch. It was approved that same day. So, from start to finish it took us about five weeks.

When I look back on it, that timeframe seems to be the norm—four to six weeks from the first moment of getting the idea in preparatory motion to getting the approval.

20

The size of the risk

Suppose for a moment that your boss is a real genuine son-of-a-bitch.

Suppose your boss believes 'if it ain't broken, don't try to fix it.'

Suppose your boss likes to belittle employees in public, particularly those employees who have some initiative.

Suppose your boss takes enjoyment in firing people.

Suppose your boss doesn't like you. Heck, your boss might have never even muttered your name, or has never even given you a kind look.

Suppose your boss doesn't like change, change of any kind. In fact, your boss abhors change.

Suppose your boss doesn't like ideas. Your boss has an attitude against somebody else's ideas.

Yep, your boss is your Supreme Court.

Should you even risk presenting an idea to your Supreme Court, who has gained notoriety among employees for having the disposition of a Hanging Judge.

The answer is yes.

The answer is yes for two reasons:

1. **You're going to be fully prepared.** Over the years, some employees have probably presented an idea or two to the Hanging Judge. I can guarantee you that you're far more prepared than those well-meaning, but woefully unprepared employees. Heck, your mean son-of-a-bitch boss probably dismissed the idea with the first objection. That won't happen to you, that's for sure.

2. **Because you're prepared, you're going to get at least a modicum of respect.** If you prepared yourself to the level that I did when I saw Leonard Lavin, then you will *gain* respect from your boss. It might be begrudging respect, but any type of new respect is *gained respect*.

For those two reasons, you would be taking little or no risk in presenting your idea (even a crazy idea) to your boss.

If your boss stamps your idea 'Approved,' that's terrific. Run with it.

If your boss stamps your idea 'Not Approved,' that's

not a crusher. Most likely, that tough boss has a new-found respect for you.

Maybe, just maybe, the tough-as-nails boss thinks you're okay and treats you accordingly. The boss might even show a willingness to approve the next idea.

21

Working for non-profits &

Other great causes

A number of years ago, a great friend of mine, Ralph, was really suffering.

Here was his dilemma:

1. He was past retirement age when his business went broke.

2. While the business was dying, he tried to prop it up with credit card debt and his retirement savings.

3. His wife developed dementia. She would need some type of care.

4. My friend fully retired, cut expenses, and became the full-time caregiver of his wife.

5. Being a fulltime caregiver showed real signs of stressful aging within six months. It looked like he might not last another six months.

6. He was at a loss at what to do. He was trying to survive each day and didn't have the luxury of thinking how to fix his plight.

7. Add to this that my friend didn't like to discuss personal issues. And he could be stubborn about that.

So, I decided to do a variation of an intervention.

This wasn't going to be the type of intervention where friends and family would gather and try to convince an alcoholic to get help. Nope, this was going to be one-on-one, my friend and me.

I met my friend for a cup of coffee. It was at the coffee shop that I made my presentation. My presentation was titled: Saving Ralph.

See if this looks familiar. The format was the very same I used to get an approval from my Supreme Court. In this situation, I used it to save a friend.

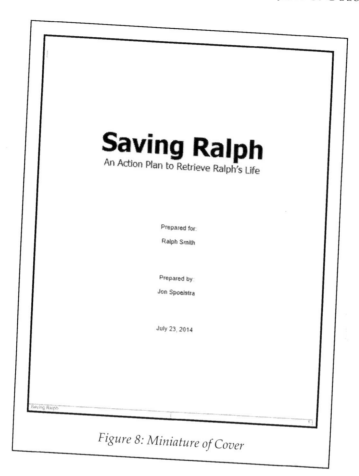

Saving Ralph
An Action Plan to Retrieve Ralph's Life

Prepared for:

Ralph Smith

Prepared by:

Jon Spoelstra

July 23, 2014

Figure 8: Miniature of Cover

Yep, this was a proposal in a business format that my buddy would understand. My wife and my sister had done all the homework on how to ease Ralph's burdens. This included finding an adult daycare center for his wife, inexpensive transportation for her and other self-help items.

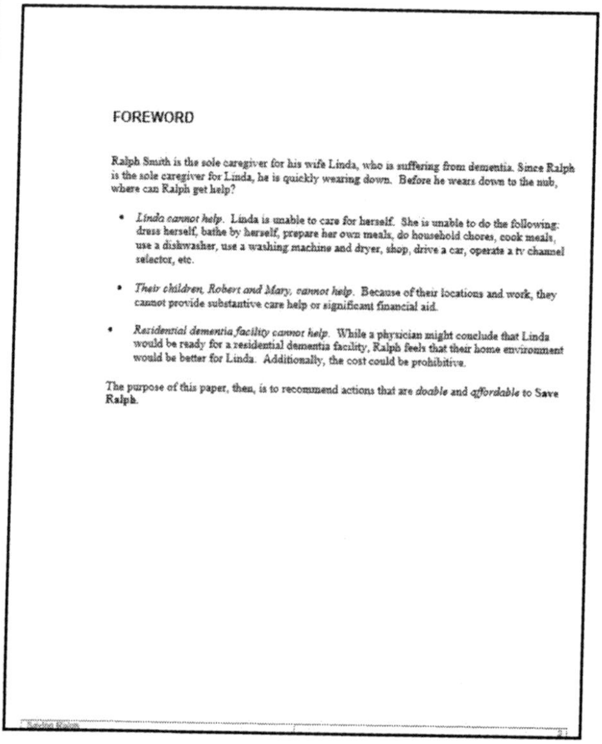

FOREWORD

Ralph Smith is the sole caregiver for his wife Linda, who is suffering from dementia. Since Ralph is the sole caregiver for Linda, he is quickly wearing down. Before he wears down to the nub, where can Ralph get help?

- *Linda cannot help.* Linda is unable to care for herself. She is unable to do the following: dress herself, bathe by herself, prepare her own meals, do household chores, cook meals, use a dishwasher, use a washing machine and dryer, shop, drive a car, operate a tv channel selector, etc.

- *Their children, Robert and Mary, cannot help.* Because of their locations and work, they cannot provide substantive care help or significant financial aid.

- *Residential dementia facility cannot help.* While a physician might conclude that Linda would be ready for a residential dementia facility, Ralph feels that their home environment would be better for Linda. Additionally, the cost could be prohibitive.

The purpose of this paper, then, is to recommend actions that are *doable* and *affordable* to **Save Ralph.**

Figure 9: Miniature of Foreword Section.

CONCEPT

Saving Ralph means creating weekly time modules where he can separate himself from the continuous pressure of care giving.

This can be done three ways:

1. **Adult Day Care: Saving Ralph three days a week.** This is affordable and flexible. Linda could spend as few as 3-4 hours per visit or up to 12 hours per visit. She could visit one day a week or every day a week. We recommend Geatog as the Adult Day Care facility for Linda. The cost is $85 a day.

ADULT DAY CARE COSTS

Hours/visit	Per Day	2 x week	3 x week	6 x per month	12 x per month
5	$67.50	$135.00	$202.50	$540.00	$810.00
8-12	$85.00	$170.00	$255.00	$680.00	$1,020.00

There is a "breaking in" period for Linda where she would attend a couple of 3-hour sessions to get comfortable with the facility. Once Linda becomes familiar with the facility, it is recommended that she would spend a **three days per week 8-hours-per-day** at the adult day care. The cost per month is $1,020.

(These can be *complete* days because once Linda becomes a regular at the *facility* Ralph doesn't even have to drive to drop off and pick up Linda from the facility. Ralph can use *Dribbet Life Service* to transport Linda door-to-door-to-and-from the facility for just $5/day.)

2. **In-home care: Saving Ralph one half-day per week.** This is a bit more expensive on an hourly basis, but is important part of the mix. We recommend an in-home service, **Visiting Angels,** to help take care of Linda.

In a 4-hour session per week, Visiting Angels can do any of the following:

a. Meal preparation.
b. Light housekeeping.
c. Personal hygiene assistance.
d. Bathing assistance.
e. Dressing assistance.
f. Grooming.
g. Walking.
h. Companionship.

Saving Ralph

Figure 10: Miniature of Concept Section.

There is a minimum of 4-hours per visit and the cost is $23 per hour or $92 per visit.

IN-HOME CARE COSTS

Hours/Visit	Per Day	1 x week	4 x per month
4	$92	$92.00	$368.00

3. **Dinner preparation: Saving Ralph the time to prepare dinners five nights a week.** We recommend **Meals-on-Wheels** to prepare and deliver dinner meals five days a week. Meals-on-Wheels is a time-saver, a stress reliever and extremely affordable. The mission of the Meals-on-Wheels people is to enrich the lives of seniors and assist them in maintaining independence by making nutritious food, social contacts and other resources accessible.

MEALS-ON-WHEELS COSTS

Meals	Per Day	5 x week	20 x per month
2	$6	$30.00	$120.00

DAYS SAVED

With this recommendation, Ralph would be saving *three full 8-hour days per week* not including the time saved by not preparing dinners:

RALPH'S HOURS NOT CONSUMED BY CARE GIVING

Service	Events/Week	Hours/Event	Hours/Week
Geripa	3	8	24
Visiting Angels	1	4	4
Meals-on-Wheels	5	NA	5
TOTALS	9		**33**

The time saved for Ralph is HUGE. He could live a more normal life than he has been for the past two years. This 33-hour reduction would dramatically reduce his stress levels.

COST

COST TO GIVE RALPH 33 HOURS PER WEEK

Service	Events/Week	Hours/Event	Hours/Week	Cost/Event	Cost/Week	Cost/Month
Geripa	3	8	24	$85	$255	$1,020
Visiting Angels	1	4	4	92	$92	$368
Meals-on-Wheels	5	NA	5	6	$30	$120
TOTALS	9		33		$377	$1,508

Saving Ralph   4

Figure 11: Miniature of second page in Concept Section.

RATIONALE

If Ralph Smith was hired as a professional caregiver to help Linda, he would put in his eight hour day—doing a terrific job—then go home for the balance of his day. As a professional caregiver, Ralph would work five days a week, 50 weeks a year, with two weeks paid vacation and a bunch of paid holidays.

Ralph, however, has not been hired as a professional caregiver—he is Linda's husband—and by default, has become Linda's fulltime caregiver. His workday doesn't end after eight hours. In fact, it continues for 16 more hours. That's like three work shifts a day, every day, every week, every month, every year. What makes it even more difficult is that Linda has severe difficulty in sleeping at night and will wake up Ralph 3-6 times a night to plead for more sleeping medication.

Ralph used to work out at the gym on a regular basis. He used to play golf regularly. He used to garden regularly. All of his activities have been eliminated because of his 24-hour care giving responsibilities.

It's naive to think that Ralph—or any human for that matter—can maintain that schedule. Something has to give. If he keeps up the same pace, the something that will give is Ralph.

The solution is, of course, to lighten Ralph's load.

There are two primary ways to lighten Ralph's load:

1. In-home care.
2. Out-of-the-house care.

The most effective way to lighten Ralph's load is option #2. Option #1 is important, but it doesn't remove Linda from the premises. With Option #1 for Ralph to get a respite, he would have to leave the house.

Option #2, however, removes Linda from the house by enrolling Linda in an adult day care facility. We recommend that for a minimum of eight hours a day three days a week.

What could Ralph do in that eight hour day?

- He might go to the gym on a regular basis.
- He might play golf.
- He might garden.
- He might take in a movie.
- He might have lunch with friends.
- He might just take a nice long nap uninterrupted.

Figure 12: Miniature of Rationale Section.

PROBLEMS

Q. What if Linda refuses to go to the adult daycare facility?

A. This is really not her option. As her caregiver, Ralph decided that this is the proper steps for her well being and *his* well being. She won't be able to understand the decision, but she is not the caregiver.

The transition to going to an adult daycare center varies per person. Most often, there is nervousness and sometimes tears in the early visits, but that soon disappears when the client becomes more comfortable with the facility.

*Q. What if Linda becomes **highly emotional** about going to the adult daycare facility?*

A. Again, the adult daycare center is not her option; it's her caregiver's. The main purpose of the adult daycare center is to give Ralph some regularly planned time every week on his own. Dementia experts have said that without that time that a caregiver will certainly be endangered.

Ralph has to be firm on this issue. He is the caregiver, not Linda.

Q. What if Linda becomes highly emotional about the once-a-week in-home care?

A. The Visiting Angel (or other in-home care) is not her option; it's her caregiver's. It would not be unusual for Linda to feel a bit nervous about this. The first time that a Visiting Angel come to the home, Ralph might stay in the house for awhile. But in subsequent visits, Ralph should not stay in the house. Linda needs to build a bond with the Visiting Angel.

Q. What if Linda wants Ralph to be at the adult day care facility while she is there?

A. The answer is absolutely not. The owner of Gentog feels strongly that Linda needs to adjust to the facility and its employees and clients. If Ralph is at the facility, it will just hurt chances of a successful transition for Linda.

Figure 13: Miniature of Rationale Section.

You get the idea. My proposal to Ralph was the very same format I used to get permission to use satellite transmissions for our radio broadcasts or to get an outfield wall that was the widest TV in the world.

I sent a copy of this proposal to both of his adult kids. Part of the plan was that the kids had to buy 'scholarships' for Ralph's wife for the adult daycare.

Ralph's background was as a businessman. He responded to the proposal as a businessman would.

He accepted all the terms. In other words, I had received his approval for him to enhance his life, probably even extending it by years.

Things have worked out for Ralph. He's in his mid-80s, his wife still goes to adult daycare every day, and he and I have lunch about once a month just to have a few laughs about the good old days.

22

Choices

You didn't get to choose your DNA.

Nor did you get to choose the style or how you got to spend your childhood years.

You do, however, get to choose what to do next. You may choose not to use The Outrageous Approval Tool.

Or, you may have a disruptive idea that is starting to burn inside you. You'd like to breathe life into that idea. You may have to get approval from your boss. If that's the case, use The Outrageous Approval Tool to help in the preparation.

Then, make your pitch.

I'm betting you'll get your idea approved.

You'll have a blast.

You'd be entering a new phase of life—getting approvals for anything you want to do.

23
Thank You

It's fun to see a tough boss approve a crazy idea. So, for that reason alone, thank God for tough bosses.

I'm thankful for all the tough bosses I've faced—maybe not so much at the time. These tough bosses provided me the grit to grind out an approval.

I want to thank all the tough bosses I've faced (and some not so tough): Frank VanLear, Bob Hamilton, Norm Sonju, John Y. Brown, Harry Mangurian, Larry Weinberg, Harry Glickman, Paul Allen, Bob Wussler, Peter Bynoe, Bertram Lee, David Stern, Alan Aufzien, Jerry Cohen, David Gerstein, Joe Taub, Henry Taub, Peter Guber, Hank Stickney, Ken Stickney, Paul Schaeffer, and Bill Luby.

I also want to thank non-boss execs who influenced me along the way in my developing The Outrageous Approval Tool whether they knew it or not: Wayne Malone, Leonard Lavin, Steve Pettise, Donald Trump and Darrell Rutter.

Then there are the folks in the pit with me at various stops in using The Outrageous Approval Tool. Thank you: Berlyn Hodges, Sue Miller, Mick Dowers, Ken Bartell, Ken Wilson, Terri Thornton & Tom McDonald at the Portland Trail Blazers; Jim Lampariello, Ray Schaetzle and Jim Leahy at the New Jersey Nets; Howie Nuchow, Steve DeLay, & Jim Bailey at Mandalay Baseball Properties; Scott Sonju, Brent Stehlik & Marcia Steinberg at Frisco RoughRiders; and Bob Murphy and Eric Deutsch at the Dayton Dragons.

Lastly, I thank my family for having the patience of tolerating me when I was severely preoccupied with creating a plan to get an approval from my Supreme Court at that time. So, thank you Lisa, my wife of many, many years, and daughter Monica Spoelstra Metz, who owns her own business where I'm sure she's faced a Supreme Court or two, and son Erik Spoelstra, the head coach of the Miami Heat, who faces a Supreme Court every game known as opponents.

24
Pigs that fly

"That'll work when pigs fly," said one of my first bosses when I approached him with an idea I had.

"That'll work when pigs fly," said other bosses along the way. In fact, if I didn't hear that phrase or something akin to it, I would start to think that the idea wasn't of the breakthrough variety.

Maybe you've heard that phrase muttered about one of your ideas. Treasure that moment. You're on the brink of a really important idea.

So, let's salute to those pigs flying all over the place.

25

Where to get the ideas

There have been times—although rare—when an idea just floats through the air and lodges somewhere in my brain, eventually popping up in my consciousness. I then feel inspired.

Most of my ideas, however, are created through a process. No magic here, these ideas are human-made.

To make these ideas, I use the coolest hack. That's right, a shortcut to ideas. I've been using it for a long time.

I sat down and wrote a step-by-step how-to on this hack to creating those human-made ideas. To make it more fun, I wrote it in the style of a business fable.

It will take you about an hour to read it and fully understand the system.

Is it worth it?

What's *one* great idea worth to you? What's *a lot of great ideas* worth to you?

The publication of *Pigs-that-Fly Hack* is a couple of months away. Just send me an email and I'll let you know when it's available.

Send to *findjon@msn.com* In the subject line type in *Pigs-that-Fly HACK*

26

Help somebody you don't know

Thank you for reading this Advanced Reader Copy of *Get Your Ideas Approved*.

It's my hope that you approved of *Approved*, and that it will indeed be helpful to you in the future.

If you enjoyed this book, I—and probably somebody you don't know—would appreciate your feedback.

As a reader, I find feedback essential in choosing whether to buy a book or not. There have been plenty of times where I was delighted with a book that a reviewer recommended.

So, a review of this book could inspire somebody to read it and help somebody get something approved by their boss. That's paying it forward, which is always a rewarding thing to do.

Please leave a review at Amazon.com.

If you want to leave me a personal message, my email is *findjon@msn.com*.

A surprise
bonus for you

"Any book about getting ideas approved should include a some chapters from *Marketing Outrageously Redux*," said my wife Lisa.

As usual, she was right. Of course.

"Good idea," I said. Here are the first few chapters of *Marketing Outrageously Redux*. Enjoy.

Ground rule #1: If you aren't willing to take a few risks in marketing, become a bean counter.

Chapter 1

Do You Have the Guts?

Right off the bat, I'm asking you to do something.

It's easy. Look at the years listed below. I want you to circle one of those years. Pick the year that was important to you: it could be the year you got married, or got a new job, or started a company. Something important. Go ahead and circle it.

1969	1982
1970	1990
1973	1991
1974	2001
1975	2007
1980	2008
1981	2009

Now I'd like you to repeat the exercise. Circle another

year that was important to you. Go ahead, mark up the book with another circle.

Those years listed are the years that the federal government designated as official recession years. Those are the hard times. Those are the times that get men and women to shake in their boots. But, take a look, you've circled two of those years as important milestone years for you.

Greatest Successes in a Bad Economy

When I first wrote *Marketing Outrageously*, I realized that my greatest successes were in a crummy economy. That made me pause. Why were my greatest personal successes in a bad economy? That wasn't logical. I looked at my performance in the years with a good economy. I wasn't lousy; in fact, I did well. After thinking it through, I realized that it was more difficult to distinguish myself in a great economy. Heck, even the dummies did well in a great economy. It was a rotten economy that provided the *best opportunity to shine*.

Sure, I had some terrific successes in a good economy, but I had outrageous successes when the economy was deemed awful by the federal government. So, I came to a simple conclusion: always (always, always) market your product as if it is a lousy economy. In other words, always (that's right, always) market outrageously. After all, if it works in a bad economy, why in all Billy Hell wouldn't you market outrageously in a good economy?

What's Outrageous About Outrageous?

You may now be wondering, "What does he mean by outrageous? And why would any responsible businessperson want to market outrageously?" It's a good question, and one that deserves a thoughtful and detailed answer. That's why I'm writing this book.

For the long answer, you need to read the whole book. This will give you plenty of good examples of outrageous marketing and the reasons it works, along with some useful pointers and guidelines about how to do it. And as you read and enjoy the book, you'll find at the end of each chapter some questions that will remind you of what you're learning. They are easy questions. They are no-brainer questions. They're outrageous questions. You can look up most of the answers in the book. Some of the answers, however, aren't in the book. You have to come up with them by applying the principles of Marketing Outrageously to your own business. You can skip them and go to the next chapter if you prefer. But if you read them and think about them, you'll learn more about Marketing Outrageously.

Okay, for you impatient types who want an easy, if incomplete, short answer, I'll give you several. Each is a partial answer that tells you something about Marketing Outrageously without giving away the whole thing—the way the seven legendary blind men described the elephant.

- Marketing Outrageously is fun.

- Marketing Outrageously is politically incorrect.

- Marketing Outrageously is using your imagination.

- Marketing Outrageously is being willing to be laughed at.

- Marketing Outrageously is putting revenue first and everything else second.

- Marketing Outrageously is dropping your assumptions and starting over with a fresh point of view.

- Marketing Outrageously is the opposite of marketing safely—but it may be the only truly safe way to market.

Okay, I can hear you. You're still asking, "What does he mean, 'Marketing Outrageously'?" It's time for another example.

What Desperate Men Do

Their backs were clearly against the wall, and desperate times called for desperate measures. In this case, their desperate measure was summoning me.

"They" were the seven owners of the New Jersey Nets—the Secaucus Seven, as the local newspapers called them, as in the Seven Dwarfs, not the Magnificent Seven. These guys had owned the Nets for fourteen years, during which the team had been consistently lousy. They usually broke even, but they could never make any real money.

Being able to break even was due mainly to NBA economics. Since 1983, there had been a cap on team salaries. With fixed expenses thus limited, the teams that prospered were those that generated the most revenue. Some teams wisely spent their limit on great players who drew fans to the arenas. Others, like the Nets, put their money into underachievers and malcontents.

In the early 1990s, the Nets were more dismal than ever. Player contracts were skyrocketing, but the Nets still couldn't get people to come to their games. Now the Nets could be really awful and lose a lot of money in the process—$4 to $5 million a season. Even if you're very rich, losing that kind of money isn't much fun.

The owners tried deeply discounting thousands and thousands of tickets. It didn't work. They tried giving away tens of thousands of tickets. The more they gave away, the more people stopped buying tickets, even discounted tickets.

"Look at this," one owner said. He handed me an empty milk carton. On the side was an offer: "Milk the Nets for $4." For just $4, you could buy a $20 ticket to see a game against Michael Jordan and the Chicago Bulls or the Nets' cross-river rivals, the New York Knicks.

"They used to have a picture of missing kids. The milk company told us they found more missing kids than we sold tickets.

"We've tried everything, and we've failed. We can't move the team because of our lease with the arena. There would be huge penalties. We need your ideas on how to get people to go to our games."

An Outrageous Plan

Even though the Nets were lousy, I felt we could boost their revenue with some unconventional marketing. I wrote a seventy-page marketing recommendation and sent a copy to each owner.

Here are the high points:

1. **Ignore Manhattan.** We would ignore the siren call of nearby Manhattan, where basketball fans cheered for the Knicks or nobody, and market to northern New Jersey, the eighth largest market in the United States.

2. **Market the other guys.** We would market

the Nets on the backs of their opponents. Instead of trying to drum up hometown loyalty for a lousy team, we would publicize appearances of our opponents' superstars, like Michael Jordan, Shaquille O'Neal, Charles Barkley, and Patrick Ewing.

3. **Families were our niche.** We would market not our players, who were mediocre at best, nor our game, which was forgettable, but family entertainment. We would make attending a Nets game an event to remember and talk about and look forward to, whether the team won or not.

A week after I mailed out my plan, we met in New Jersey. Here's the first thing one owner said:

"When I read your marketing recommendation, I got furious. In fact, I had to walk around the block two times just to cool down. Everything you recommended went against what I believed in. After I walked around the block a few more times, I started to think that this was absolutely brilliant. But I also thought it was totally outrageous. This is really Marketing Outrageously."

That's not the first time I had heard that term applied to my marketing concepts. In fact, I had gotten used to it. If I didn't hear it, I would begin to suspect something was wrong.

I told the owners, "It may sound outrageous, but it

isn't. It's just unusual. But it'll work—if you have the guts."

"We've got the guts," the owner said, puffing out his chest. "But what if these ideas don't work?"

"Sell the team," I said.

I wasn't trying to be glib. It was just that if these ideas didn't work, nothing would. Fortunately, there were always people who wanted to buy NBA teams, even miserable ones.

Cut to the chase: The concepts worked. Gloriously so. In three seasons, the revenue from paid tickets went up from $5 million to $17 million. Local sponsorships ballooned from $400,000 to $7 million. Most important for the Secaucus Seven, the market value of the team grew from $40 million to more than $120 million. Two years after I left the team, they sold it for a reported $140 million.

My Most Outrageous Weakness

Let's jump ahead a few more years to another NBA team I consulted for.

"All you care about is increasing revenue," the president of that team said to me.

I nodded.

"You don't care about the ramifications that has on other departments, like the box office. The box office people are now way overworked."

I nodded again, smiling.

"You don't care that our pay scale gets all out of

whack. The marketing people and salespeople are making more and more."

Again I nodded.

"That's a weakness," he said. "You're too one-dimensional, too focused on increasing revenue."

I agreed. To this president, who ran a hapless pro sports team, he was right. To the owners who brought me in, however, being so focused on revenue was a tremendous strength.

I've got a simplistic way of looking at success in business. I believe all major corporate problems stem from inadequate revenue. I've never seen a company in trouble from having too much revenue.

This book is about what I do best—increasing revenue by marketing.

What's So Outrageous About Marketing?

Corporations often try to make up for a lack of revenue by means other than marketing. Here are three trendy ways:

1. **The Investment Way and the Borrow It Way.** Somewhere along the way, the words "revenue" and "investment" or "loan" somehow came to mean the same thing. Need cash? You can raise revenue, or you can raise investment dollars or just borrow it. Investment is cool, because you can live in Oz. You can float wild promises and predictions and rake in millions on

the stock market. Sooner or later, of course, the company will indeed have to *raise revenue and make a profit*—but that's for somebody else to worry about. You long ago cashed in on your stock options and drove away in your new Maserati.

2. **The Edward Scissorhands Approach.** Even in the best of times, companies should always be undergoing minor liposuction. Unfortunately, some companies look to a present-day Edward Scissorhands, the movie character that had multiple snapping scissors as hands, as the cost-cutting role model for increasing profits in the short term. These companies even go further; they crank up the chainsaws and cut away some fat, along with a lot of muscle and gizzard and bone. Wall Street loves this approach. The more blood on the floor, the better.

3. **Let's Make a Deal.** This is a popular solution with larger corporations. Instead of increasing revenue by marketing, it's far easier just to merge or buy somebody. With a couple of signatures, the CEO can make it look like he doubled revenue in a blink. (Let's see you do that, marketers!) A merger looks terrific to the Wall Street folks, and it usually brings the CEO enormous bonuses.

Such bonuses should be considered blood money. The merger is usually paid with the salaries of the thousands of employees who are laid off. The merged company is "reengineered," and the new mantra is "synergy."

Synergy, by the way, doesn't work in growing the new company's revenues through marketing. "Synergy" is just a word used to justify increasing revenue by acquisition, a smoke-and-mirrors solution for the CEO who wants to head straight to his bank. Instead of "synergy," think "parachute"—as in "golden parachute"—for the CEO and a handful of other top executives.

Let's say a company does all three of these things to increase profit. What will it have to do next? Eventually, the company will have to raise revenue by marketing.

That's what this book is about: raising revenue by marketing. It sounds a bit old-fashioned—and it is, because it deals with marketing fundamentals. But to raise revenue in staggering amounts, which is the aim of Marketing Out-rageously, you have to twist and pull and stretch those fundamentals. You have to push the envelope.

Raising your revenue a little bit each year is like taking steps backwards.

When you twist and pull and stretch marketing fundamentals, you're entering the world of Marketing Outrageously.

Is Outrageous Dangerous?

You might say, "I'm sort of a conservative person. Outrageous sounds dangerous to me. Can I get fired doing this stuff?"

I would say to you, "It depends."

"It depends? Depends on what?"

"How big is your company?" I would ask.

If the company you work for is a mega-corporation, then Marketing Outrageously might be hazardous to your immediate health. You see, the outrageous ideas and strategies in this book are not, by themselves, dangerous. However, they are different, and in a mega-corporation, just being different can be risky. An outrageous marketing idea presented in writing might be considered a professional suicide note. It's far safer for your job security to do plain-vanilla marketing. No staggering increases in revenues for you; play for a safe, steady 5 percent.

Unfortunately, the man with the hood and the tall axe will eventually come for you. He'll direct you to stretch out your neck. "Sorry," he'll say, "5 percent increases aren't good enough. One of your competitors is using outrageous marketing and taking huge bites out of your market share." So, if you work for a mega-corporation, you might as well market outrageously. It may seem scary at first, but it's not as scary as that character with the axe. After you get over the initial shock, you'll learn safe ways to use the principles of Marketing Outrageously. And you'll look like a genius.

For a smaller company, outrageous isn't dangerous at all—in fact, *it's far more perilous to market conservatively.* To conserve means to save—as in saving yourself to become a late-night snack for a bigger, revenue-hungry competitor.

Outraging the Naysayer

I've marketed in great economic times. I've also marketed in awful economic times, with unemployment and inflation soaring. I've marketed in the Rust Belt when it seemed that every business was moving south (will the last company leaving town please turn out the lights?). There are two things that are consistent about marketing, whether in the Golden Age or the Toilet Age:

1. Naysayers live here. It doesn't matter what the economy is doing. Naysayers are always there, like flies in .

A friend of my daughter spent some time in . When he got back, we were on our deck discussing his experiences. I asked him what one image stuck in his mind. I was thinking about the Great Wall or the or something like that. He said, "The flies."

"The flies?" I asked.

"Flies," he said. "They're *everywhere*."

"That can't be," I said. "I read that during the Cultural Revolution Mao asked every man, woman, and child to catch 100 flies. They wanted to eradicate flies from their country. There were a billion people living in at that time. If each man, woman, and child did indeed catch 100 flies, then there would have been one hundred billion flies caught and killed!"

"Well," my daughter's friend said, "Maybe there

were 100 billion flies hiding somewhere. Now they're out of hiding. They're everywhere!"

Naysayers and flies always survive. As found out with flies, you can't get rid of them. Same with naysayers.

If it's a lousy economy, the naysayer will say, "We can't do that marketing outrageous stuff. We've got to be conservative. We've got to be careful."

When the biggest bull is running around in the economy, the naysayer will say, "We don't need to do that marketing outrageous stuff. We can afford to be conservative. We can afford to be careful."

These naysayers—regardless of a good or bad economy—want to label Marketing Outrageously as reckless and foolish. It's not. As I have said, it's just different. When have you found a naysayer who liked something different?

So, if you choose to employ the principles of Marketing Outrageously, prepare yourself for the naysayer. He'll be there, no doubt about it. That, by itself, isn't so bad or even dangerous. In fact, as we'll see later, having naysayers can be an advantage.

2. Marketing Outrageously works marvelously. You would think that Marketing Outrageously would work better in a bullish economy. Not so. Marketing Outrageously works equally well whether the economy is sluggish or booming. In this book, I'll give you examples of both.

I'll use examples from the world of sports, of course, because that's my world and the bulk of my experience. I think you'll find them entertaining, whether you're a sports fan or not—although you should be especially thankful I didn't come from the world of portable toilet sales. But I'll also provide examples of businesses large and small that have nothing to do with sports—unless cutthroat competition is your game of choice.

The beginning and end of each chapter

At the beginning of each chapter, I tell a little anecdote from my experiences in the NBA and other sports, or sometimes just a story about something unusual that's happened to me. This is just my way of easing you into the chapter—my "slippery slide" (more on this later).

But once you've read it, don't stop. Keep reading. Dig into the real meat of Marketing Outrageously, because I have a little test waiting for you at the end of each chapter. In fact, here's the first test:

An Outrageous Test

To help you in adapting these principles to your company, I throw in "A Simple Test You Can Take" at the end of each chapter. There's a easy way to grade this test. You don't send in your answers for a grade. If you answer the questions, you get an "A." If you just skip over the test, you don't just flunk the test, you flunk the book. So do me and yourself a favor. Just take the test and let the ideas flow.

Answer the following multiple-choice question:

1. I want to

    a. Increase the revenue of my company dramatically.

    b. Steal market share from the leaders in my field.

    c. Increase my own compensation.

    d. Increase the compensation of all the good marketing and salespeople in my company.

    e. All of the above.

    f. None of the above.

    g. Use this information to help downsize my company.

Answers

1. If you answered "e," you did terrific! You scored 150 out of a possible 100. Better yet, you'll enjoy this book

and learn to apply principles of Marketing Outrageously. When you do, you'll see that they work. Your company will grow. You'll be a hero, you'll be paid a king's ransom, and your employees will consider you a saint.

If your answer was "f," I'm not sure why you've read this far. I'll award you an "incomplete." If you manage to finish the book, come back and take this test again.

If you answered "g," turn in your test and walk out the door. You must be a financial type who will be trying to learn the principles of Marketing Outrageously so that you can be a little knowledgeable when you try to kill company growth. Well, reading this book won't work for you. The book will just confirm your belief that all marketing people are crazy.

Ground rule #2: When you aim for the top, you make important progress by just the aiming.

Chapter 2

What's It Gonna Take?

We don't set out to produce lousy movies," Peter Guber told me. Peter is the former chairman of Sony Pictures and now chairman of Mandalay Entertainment. Peter has so many Oscars and Emmys and other awards that he's run out of wall space to display them.

"The producer and director and writer don't start out thinking they're going to create a lousy movie," Peter said. "The actors certainly don't, either. After all, a real bomb could set their careers back. It sometimes just happens that even truly talented people make a bomb. For whatever reason, the chemistry just doesn't work. Then there are other times when the chemistry works perfectly, even with a small budget, and everything is wonderful and profitable."

That got me thinking of my line of work. There's not a pro sports team owner I know of who starts out with the thought of creating a lousy team, no general manager who sets out to get ripped in the media or booed by the fans. Yet many of them have turned out some unbelievably lousy teams. Imagine how lousy they could have been if they had planned it.

There are thirty teams in the National Basketball Association. Of these thirty, only four or five, at the most, are thinking during the off-season about winning the championship. These four or five teams ask themselves, "What's it going to take to win it all this year?"

Pat Riley, president of the Miami Heat, thinks championship. If the Heat goes to the NBA finals and gets beat, Riley considers the season unsuccessful. It's win the championship or nothing. There's no question that that was what he was thinking when he maneuvered to get superstars LeBron James and Chris Bosh to join Heat superstar Dwyane Wade. There are a handful of teams that think the same way. For the 2010–11 season, that handful is the Los Angeles Lakers, the Boston Celtics, the Orlando Magic and the San Antonio Spurs. Other team executives and coaches think about improving their record a bit or advancing one more round in the playoffs.

Hooray for those who think, plot, and dream to win it all this year.

The Question

Do you know anyone who starts out with the thought of creating a lousy company?

Don't spend much time thinking about that—you won't think of any. Sure, you know some lousy companies, but nobody started out with the concept of creating them that way.

I don't have any easy solution for those movie producers about not producing lousy movies, or the pro sports team owner on how not to produce a loser, or the businessperson on how not to create a lousy company. But I do have one suggestion.

Learn to ask this question: "What's it going to take?"

Most businesspeople are thinking, "How can we make our budget numbers?" or "How can we improve our profit over last year?" They are asking the wrong question.

What if you asked the following question at your company: "What's it going to take to be the best company in our industry *this year?*"

You don't have to be a CEO or a business owner to ask this kind of question. You could ask, "What's it going to take to become the best marketing department in the industry *this year?*" or "What's it going to take to be the best department in our company *this year?*"

I know how difficult it is to answer that question. I've asked it many times. Sometimes I've just asked myself, because it can seem too outrageous to ask anyone else. Sometimes I've asked others, even though if they'd been carrying guns I'd probably be dead. But you have to ask it, because that's the only way to come up with truly outrageous marketing ideas.

I'll give you an example. In the late 1980s, I was general manager of the Portland Trail Blazers. Even though

I didn't have the authority to draft or trade players, I could call meetings with those who did. I assembled the coaches and player personnel managers and asked the question, "What's it gonna take to win the championship this year?"

Logically, it was a foolish question. This was the era when Magic Johnson and Kareem Abdul-Jabbar were leading the Los Angeles Lakers to regular championships. When the Lakers didn't win, Larry Bird and the Boston Celtics did. Lining up to cut in on the Lakers and Celtics were Michael Jordan and the Chicago Bulls. So how stupid was my question, "What's it going to take to win the NBA championship *this year?*"

On paper, we didn't have a chance; in our minds, less than no chance. We were, however, a pretty good team. We had won fifty-three games the year before. Considering all this, I wanted us to *think* beyond what we had.

The player personnel people took the question as an insult. I could hear them thinking, "Who does this marketing guy think he is?" They fumed and grumbled for a while.

I asked the question again. "What's it going to take to win a championship this year?"

Silence. Finally, John Wetzel, an assistant coach, said, "One thing we need to do is really improve our outside shooting. We need some guy that can come off the bench and really fill it up."

"*Two* shooters," said Rick Adelman, another assistant. "When we get to the playoffs, we can't run our fast break as much, and the middle gets clogged up. We need *two* reliable shooters coming off the bench."

We talked for two hours. Head Coach Mike Shuler was enthusiastic, salivating over the thought of somehow acquiring two bona fide outside shooters. We made a list of players who might be available. We came away from the meeting with assignments for each of us to start making inquiries with other teams.

Later, Rick Adelman told me, "I've been in a lot of player personnel meetings over the years, and this was the best. We actually talked about winning a championship and what that would take."

Did I think we had a chance to win the championship that year? Not really. But I knew we had no chance to improve unless we set the target higher than what was comfortable.

Beyond the Question

Seven years later, as president of the New Jersey Nets, I found myself asking the same question. I had no voice in choosing the players—my expertise is raising revenue in staggering amounts to pay for these guys—but I thought I'd ask anyway.

At the time, the Nets were a hapless team with a hapless past and a hapless future. The team had won only thirty games the year before and lost fifty-two. So picture the reaction from Willis Reed, our general manager, when I asked, "What's it going to take to win a championship this year?"

Willis just stared at me. The fact that Willis is one of the five nicest men I've ever met probably saved me from having my head torn off. He probably wondered if I was on drugs or was just naturally crazy.

Finally, Willis said, "Sign Michael Jordan and Karl Malone and Shaquille O'Neal as free agents."

That answer, of course, was just as crazy as my question. But I persisted: "Really, what's it going to take to win the championship this year?"

"It's not possible," Willis said.

"I can accept that," I said. I knew our cast of characters. They had multiple-year contracts. Not even the master magician David Copperfield could have made them disappear in just a year. "Let me rephrase my question. What's it going to take to win the championship *next* year?"

There was some method to these crazy questions. Most player personnel people aim to improve a little bit each year. That's also the way most marketing managers think. Steady progress is good enough, they say.

Bunk, I say.

A team can always come up with legitimate-sounding reasons why it can't compete for a championship. Willis had one: "We don't have the money to make it next year, or the year after that, or the year after that."

Money, the Easy Scapegoat

Does this sound familiar? "We don't have the budget to be the best." Or "We don't have the budget to dramatically improve our market share." Or "We don't have the money to increase our revenue by staggering amounts."

Money. The reason for not competing for the championship or becoming the best company in the industry is always related to money. It's never "We don't think big enough." It's never "We don't have enough moxie." It's never "We don't have good enough ideas."

When I ask businesspeople the "What's it gonna take?" question and get the money answer, I always ask, "How much money would you need to become the best?" The answer is usually a little vague. They've never really thought about it; they're usually focused on making their budget goals or improving a little bit. But they're also a little afraid. What if they did have enough money to become the best, and they still didn't make it? It's safer to be mediocre.

When Pigs Learn to Fly

Becoming the best takes more than money; it takes thinking big from the start. When lack of money pops up, then it's time for some creative thinking. That's what Marketing Outrageously is all about—modest marketing budgets, big impact.

When Willis told me that money was the reason we couldn't compete for the NBA championship, I asked my stock question, "How much is it going to take?" Now that was a legitimate question. After all, that's what I did for a living—raise a team's revenues and profits.

Willis gave me an answer. It was more than just higher player salaries. It was a bigger scouting budget.

It was a fancier private jet the team could use to travel to road games. It was a lot of things, adding up to $5 million over budget.

The $5 million was a stretch for us, I told Willis, but if that's what it took, we'd get the money. "Now," I said, "what's it gonna take to win a championship next year?"

"Well, we'll need two superstars," Willis said. " has Michael Jordan and Scottie Pippin, the Lakers have Magic and Abdul-Jabbar, the Celtics have Bird and McHale. We've got just one—Derrick Coleman—and he won't practice with the team."

Derrick Coleman was a very talented basketball player—six foot ten, 258 pounds of pure athlete. Unfortunately, he didn't like to compete and wouldn't practice. He didn't like basketball.

"Can we count Derrick as one of those superstars?" I asked. "There's no question about his talent, but does he have the character, the work ethic, the personality?"

"Maybe as he matures he'll develop those," Willis said.

"Let's go back to my original question. What's it going to take to win a championship next year? Do we have to wait and see if Derrick grows up?" Player personnel specialists can fool themselves into mediocrity. I wanted Willis to think about what could actually be done, given the player situation. I wanted to give him a sense of urgency. Would Derrick Coleman fit into the game plan for winning the championship? Maybe he could develop character and a work ethic, but it would be around the time that pigs learned to fly.

Answering the Question

I asked Willis what it would take to make the Nets a championship team. His bottom-line answer was money. That put the ball in my court. As president of the Nets and the person in charge of coming up with the money, I had to ask myself a different question: What's it gonna take to make our marketing department the best one of them all? That could bring in the money.

Before becoming president, I was the Nets' marketing consultant for two and a half years. In my second year as consultant, I asked Jim Leahy, vice president of ticket sales, this question: "What's it gonna take for the Nets to have the best ticket sales department in all of sports?"

"All the things we can't get," Leahy said.

"Let's make a list," I said.

We closed the door to his office and sat down, Leahy at his computer.

Leahy said that the first item on the list should be a better team.

"You can't have that," I said. "We work with the product we are given. The team has been awful in the past, and its near future looks awful. We market the team we're given. Now, under these circumstances, let's come up with a list of what it's gonna take to become the best ticket sales department in all of sports this year."

Here's what we came up with:

1. **More salespeople.** is a huge market. If you picked it up and dropped it into the state of , it would be the eighth largest market in the country. It had 20,000 businesses we could count as targets. We determined that we should have one salesperson per 1,000 businesses. We had seven ticket salespeople, so we needed thirteen more. Leahy thought the owners would never approve that increase in overhead.

2. **A reasonable work environment.** Why did the Nets have only seven ticket salespeople? Because we had only seven work cubicles. The offices at that time were in the arena and there was no more available space. We would have to rent space outside the arena. "The owners will never approve that," Leahy said.
   "We're not passing judgment now on whether we can do it or not," I said. "We're just making a list of what it's going to take to have the best ticket sales department in all of sports. A reasonable work environment is one of those factors." He wrote it down on the list.

3. **Training, training, training, and when we were tired, more training.** We hired young people with little or no experience. And we

hired cheap. Homeless people made more money. However, these kids wanted to "run away and join the circus"—get into pro sports—and we had the circus.

To be successful, we could not wait for these young salespeople to get better naturally. We had to accelerate their progress.

"I can get them started with a ticket sales boot camp," I told Leahy, "but the real burden falls on your shoulders. We need to train every day."

4. **More tools for the salespeople.** Most teams have their salespeople sell just season tickets. You know, buy a ticket to all the team's games or don't buy at all. That strategy might work for a team like the Chicago Bulls, which won six championships in eight years, but for most other teams it was self-defeating. "No problem," I told Leahy, "This one is the easiest thing on the list." We had already created some very popular ticket packages the year before. We would just create some more for specific corporate targets.

5. **Big-time database marketing.** We had started to collect names of people who we knew were interested in the Nets or the

NBA. We needed to dramatically expand that effort. It would take computers and a "Database King"—somebody who would stay up nights thinking of ways to expand the list.

That list doesn't seem too intimidating, does it? Not at all. Next, I asked Leahy to swap chairs with me. I started typing on his computer. We were going to prepare a case for the Supreme Court—not the nine worthies in long robes, but the seven owners of the Nets. This document would be the key to becoming the number one ticket sales department.

We worked on the report for two days. It wasn't just typing; we needed to gather evidence. For instance, we knew the owners wouldn't agree to hire thirteen more salespeople and rent space for them without knowing the cost. We found space near the arena. We itemized the costs of salespeople, office, and phones. We projected sales. The whole report was only eight pages, but it answered every question, every objection that a naysayer could come up with. Then we rehearsed our oral presentation. We took this as seriously as if we were petitioning the real Supreme Court to save us from the lethal injection.

Our plan was approved in two weeks. A year later, we had a ticket marketing machine. A year after that, we had the best ticket sales department in all of sports. In fact, it might have been the best ticket sales department that ever was and ever will be.

It all started with just one question: "What's it gonna

take to become the best ticket marketing department in all of sports?" In the most hopeless situation you could find in sports—the New Jersey Nets—we had done it.

When You've Got Nothing

You know the one thing that most start-up companies don't have? Cash. When these start-ups think about advertising, they stop thinking about it a few seconds later. An advertising budget isn't something you think about as a start-up. Let's take this a step further. Suppose you're a start-up with little cash, and to make things worse it's a bad economy. Instead of heading for the hills, let's look at how this start-up from , took steps forward.

The entrepreneur is a guy named Gary Keller, and he formed a real estate agency named Keller Williams Realty. They started in 1983 when mortgage rates were as high as 13 percent (ouch!).

Gary Keller asked his team the question: What's it gonna take to get people to visit our houses?

Money for advertising was, of course, not there for Keller Williams. No newspaper ads for them. No radio or TV. Instead of spending money that they didn't have, they made cheap yard signs. They blanketed the nearby expressway to promote open houses during the weekend. On Monday, the city workers came by and took down all the cheap signs, but the Keller Williams mission was accomplished. They had sold houses!

The 'bandit' signs had worked. Back to making more

hand-made signs. Four years later, Keller Williams was the number- one real estate agency in .

Years later, Keller Williams offices were expanding all over the . To help increase their awareness in new territories Gary Keller asked his team: "What's it gonna take to make this company famous?"

They could have spent millions of dollars running quirky ads on the Super Bowl like Go Daddy. But Keller Williams built the business with no advertising. Instead of ads, he wrote three national bestsellers:

- *The Millionaire Real Estate Agent* (over 500,000 copies sold)

- *The Millionaire Real Estate Investor*

- *SHIFT: How Top Real Estate Agents Tackle Tough Times* (made the *New York Times, Wall Street Journal,* and *USA Today* bestseller lists)

These books have sold over 1,000,000 copies! They are, of course, the perfect example of target marketing: they made Keller Williams famous to real estate agents across the country. When Keller Williams came recruiting, it was as well known to real estate agents as the University of Texas, Southern Cal, Florida, or Notre Dame is to football prospects.

2008 and 2009 have been the roughest years in the real estate industry in 70 years. Many Realtors were downsizing as fast as they could. In that time, Coldwell Banker had lost 12 percent of its agents; Century 21 had lost 21 percent; RE/MAX had lost 12.8 percent. Keller Williams had gained 8.3 percent!

Keller Williams is the third largest real estate company in the . By the time the ink dries on this book they could be number two; they're that close. And it all started with an outrageous idea of using cheap hand-made signs instead of expensive advertising.

It's easy to ask the question, "What's it gonna take?" It's the answer that causes pain. I learned this as a consultant to troubled teams. If I asked business executives of pro sports teams, "What's it gonna take to be the best marketing department in the league this year?" I faced a lot of resistance. People would tell me in great detail why it wasn't possible. If I had debated them, I would have lost. They had hard evidence. After all, year after year they proved that what they were doing wasn't working and that there were plenty of valid reasons that it wasn't their fault.

When even the concept of asking "What's it gonna take" makes executives get into a sumo's stance, I feel like sending them to . Why ? Well, I understand they still allow lobotomies to be done. You know, drill a hole in the temple, stick in a screwdriver, stir it around, patch it up. But I'm a marketing guy, not a travel agent. I work with the product I'm given—and the people. Instead of sending them to , I get them to start making a list of what it's gonna take.

Two Small Favors

The whole purpose of this chapter is to get you to ask yourself just one question. You know the question. It depends, of course, on your situation. It could focus on your department:

What's it gonna take to be the best marketing department in our industry this year?

Or maybe it's about your company:

What's it gonna take to raise revenue in staggering amounts this year?

Here's the first favor I'll ask of you. Take the question that is most applicable to you and write it down on a 3 x 5 card. Or an envelope. Or a bar napkin. Anything you can put in your shirt pocket. Go ahead, write it down. I'll wait.

That's the first favor. The second favor's even easier. Whatever you wrote that question down on, put it in your shirt pocket. Go ahead, try it. Now, get used to that question in your shirt pocket. You need to have it there every day. You don't need to show it to anybody. This is just a little favor you are doing for me—our little secret.

Don't worry about answering that question right now. You'll come up with more and better answers as you read each chapter of this book. Believe me, the tough part isn't the answers. The tough part is asking yourself such a demanding question. Now that you've done that—and the question is tucked away safely in your shirt pocket—the rest is easy. Read on.

A Simple Test You Can Take

There are only two questions to the simple test for this chapter. Don't blow it.

1. I wrote down the question "What's it gonna take to _____ this year?" and placed it in my shirt pocket. (True/False)

2. We're already the best (department or company), so I don't need to write down that question and put it in my shirt pocket. (True/False)

Answers

1. I hope you did me that favor and circled True. If you didn't, you were probably intimidated by the question. Or you just thought it was a silly exercise. Well, first of all, I didn't ask you if the question was reasonable. All I asked you was a favor—just write down the question and put it in your shirt pocket. You may consider the question unreasonable or impossible. For now, that's irrelevant. What's relevant is that you do me the favor.

If you are truly intimidated by the question, I'm willing to back off a little bit. Let me ask you the back-up question:

What's it gonna take to _____ next year?

Notice how I'm giving you a little breathing room?

It's not this year, it's next year. Now you've got some time.

So you still have time to ace this little test for chapter 2. Go ahead, write down the question. Place it in your shirt pocket. Mark your answer True.

2. True. You don't have to write down the question and put it in your shirt pocket. All you have to do is think about the fact that some of your competitors may have written down the question, put it in their shirt pockets, and are now starting to think about how to steal some market share from you.

Can't happen? Heh, heh. Remember when General Motors had 60 percent of the automobile market? Remember when IBM dominated the computer business? When Kodak had a 90 percent share in color film? When Xerox was becoming a generic name for copying? Nobody, but nobody, thought those companies would lose their dominance.

Now, after you've thought about this, read the second question again. See if you can come up with a different answer.

P.S. What's It Gonna Take to Have Really Outrageous Customer Service?

The Dayton Dragons, a single-A minor league baseball team, started its games in 2000. For the one hundred years before that, no team in the history of minor league baseball had sold every ticket to every game during a season. That, of course, piqued my interest. What if we applied the same marketing principles that we did in the NBA to the Dayton Dragons? Why wouldn't we sell out?

We felt we could market our way to selling every seat to every game during the first season. Subsequent sellout seasons, however, required more. We needed a secret weapon. The secret weapon was outrageous customer service.

In planning before that first season, we asked ourselves one serious question: What's it gonna take to have the best customer service in all of sports? *Outrageous customer service!*

Marketing was going to deliver us sellouts in the first year; customer service was going to deliver us sellouts in the following years.

Keep in mind that the frontline troops in our customer service were mostly part-time employees like ushers and food service people. Some of the workers were retired. Many of these people had a day job. They would work a full day someplace else, and then come to work for us. If they had a bad day at work, it would be easy for them to take out their frustration with our customers.

Here's some of the things we did:

1. **Your responsibility to buy dropped ice cream.** If any employee, whether an usher or the team president, sees a fan drop an ice cream (or soda or hot dog or beer), it was

the employee's responsibility to offer to buy a replacement product right away. The usher or president would spend his or her own money and then be reimbursed at the end of the game. No receipts were necessary. That may sound too lenient, too open for scams, but if one employee was allegedly buying 200 replacement ice cream cones, we'd probably figure it out.

2. **No thick customer service manual.** Instead, we used a wall. That's right a wall. We tried to impress upon our part-time employees that they were empowered to do "whatever it takes to solve a fan's problem." That right, whatever it takes. How in the world would we explain that in real terms? A thick manual might do it, but, alas, nobody would read it. Instead, our fans could tell our part-time employees about great customer service. For instance, we got a letter from a lady who had brought her elderly mother to a game. After the game, they were slowly navigating their way out. One of the ushers asked if he could help. He helped guide them to their car a block away. That letter, blown up to poster size, went up on the wall in the employees' locker room. It joined six other letters, each one distinct

in telling how an usher helped a fan. So, when we got a new employee, we said that it was his or her responsibility to "do whatever it takes to solve a fan's problem" and for guidelines "read the wall." And then take a quick True/False quiz. That was our customer service manual.

3. **Choice tickets for free, and you get paid**. There were times that our ushers just wanted to attend one of our games as a fan. We made that possible. We had eight season tickets that we dedicated to our part-time employees. They'd sign up for the games they wanted to attend. So they wouldn't lose a payday, we also *paid them* the nights they went to the games as a fan. (There were a couple of rules here: the part-time employee just couldn't give the tickets away and not attend the game. These tickets were for the employees, their families, and friends—and they should enjoy the game with them.)

4. **Free gifts**. During the season, we would give various gifts to our ticket package buyers. You know, bobbleheads or baseballs or hats. We made sure that our part-time employees also received those gifts.

There was a lot more that we did for our part-time employees that worked our games, but you get the idea.

The results?

Well, first of all, we had a bunch of part-time employees that were an absolute delight to be with.

And we received thousands of letters and emails from fans that were enthralled with our customer service. The unusual things our employees did. Some of those things actually made the wall.

And yes, we did sell out every ticket to every game in that first year. Then the sellout string continued year after year after year. Sometime in 2011, the Dayton Dragons will break the sellout string of 814 games by the Portland Trail Blazers (from 1977–1991).

Marketing gave us that first year of sellouts. Asking "What's it gonna take to have the best customer service in all of sports?" led us to all the following years of sellouts.

Marketing Outrageously Redux
Table of Contents

About the Author

Jon Spoelstra spent most of his adult life running pro sports teams, first NBA teams and then a group of seven minor league baseball teams.

With each job, there was at least one (seemingly) off-the-wall whacky crazy idea that was a long shot for the approval of the team's owner. That's where the fun began.

Some of those approvals are featured in *Get Your Ideas Approved*. Other approvals were turned into stories in his three marketing books: *Ice to the Eskimos, Marketing Outrageously*, and *Marketing Outrageously Redux*. All of Jon's books are available on Amazon.com.

A strange thing about Approvals is that once you get one, it's even more fun to get another. Even to collect them. Start your collection today.

Made in the USA
Coppell, TX
15 October 2022